The Labyrinth

On Ariadne's Thread. Drawing by Art Glöckner.

The Labyrinth

SYMBOL OF FEAR, REBIRTH, AND LIBERATION

Helmut Jaskolski

Translated by Michael H. Kohn

Shambhala
Boston & London
1997

Shambhala Publications, Inc.
Horticultural Hall
300 Massachusetts Avenue
Boston, Massachusetts 02115
http://www.shambhala.com

Original publisher: Kreuz Verlag Stuttgart

Pages 193–194 constitute a continuation of this copyright page

9 8 7 6 5 4 3 2 1

First Edition
Printed in the United States of America

♾ This edition is printed on acid-free paper that meets
the American National Standards Institute Z39.48 Standard.
Distributed in the United States by Random House, Inc.,
and in Canada by Random House of Canada Ltd

Library of Congress Cataloging-in-Publication Data
Jaskolski, Helmut.
[Labyrinth. English]
The labyrinth: symbol of fear, rebirth, and liberation / Helmut
Jaskolski; translated by Michael H. Kohn.
p. cm.
Includes bibliographical references and index.
ISBN 1-57062-195-0 (alk. paper)
1. Labyrinths. I. Title.
BL325.L3J3713 1997   96-23353
302.2'22—dc20   CIP

For Hanna
and
to Hermann Kern
(1941–1984)
with gratitude

*Is it possible that phenomena so lacking in unity
could be named in such a unitary fashion? And yet
this, it seems to me, is the teaching left us by our
greatest learned doctors:*

OMNIS ERGO FIGURA TANTO EVIDENTIUS VERITATUM
DEMONSTRAT QUANTO APERTIUS PER DISSIMILEM
SIMILITUDINEM FIGURAM SE ESSE ET NON VERITATEM
PROBAT.

*Therefore, any figure refers more clearly to the truth
the more openly it shows, through dissimilar similari-
ty, that it is indeed a figure and not the truth.*

—UMBERTO ECO, *The Name of the Rose*

Contents

The Labyrinth

Introduction

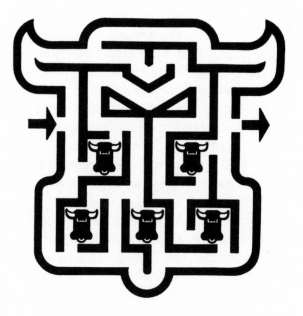

"Labyrinth of the Bulls," I read, and under that the instructions for the game: to find the way through without using any of the passages more than once and still pay a visit to each of the five bulls. Do you perhaps know what bulls have to do with labyrinths?

In Germany, where I live, the word *labyrinth* triggers a whole range of different ideas. Some people are interested in working the puzzle page of their Sunday paper; others like to relax with labyrinth-based board games or science fiction stories, and in that genre they might have encountered *The Rat in the Maze*.[1] To game players and bookworms can be added of late therapy-wise depth divers and esoteric seekers of the self. Workshops catering to this interest can be found on offer under names like "Questing in the Labyrinth of Life."

Introduction

In another quarter, culture seekers, whose temples have greyed since the time they read it, will likely recall Gustav René Hocke's book from *Rowohlts Deutsche Enzyklopädie*, which exercised a major influence in the educational scene around 1960, *Die Welt als Labyrinth: Manier und Manie in der europäischen Kunst* (The World as Labyrinth: Mode and Mania in European Art).[2] True, there was little enough to be found there in the way of concrete proofs of humanity's alleged cult of the labyrinth;[3] however, the human and cosmic symbol that people discovered in the book subsequently remained for the initiated an essential part of their intellectual trappings. At that time, Franz Kafka was recognized as the "poet of the labyrinth,"[4] and the mannerism of the Romantics was perceived as a manifestation of the labyrinthine.[5] These interpretations were supported in the art-historical realm by an exhibit whose title was an indication of the prevailing point of view: "Labyrinth: Fantastic Art from the Sixteenth Century to the Present" (Berlin, 1966–67). There was much metaphorical talk about this fantastic phenomenon, but rare were the attempts at concrete analysis.[6]

At this time, our Anglo-Saxon neighbors were approaching the labyrinth in an entirely different manner. In the traditional land of mazes and labyrinths,[7] after a period of inactivity necessitated by circumstance, there was a renaissance of the garden maze and, as an inseparable part of it, an intensified interest in all the mysteries connected with the labyrinth since the time of King Minos. It was the English sculptor Michael Ayrton who, beginning in 1956, in the wake of his mystical experience at the legendary site of the Sybilline oracle in Cumae, Italy, provided the impetus for the rediscovery of the labyrinth symbol. With his monumental maze in the American town of Arkville, he created an original paragon for the modern mind-set. *The Maze Maker* is what this new Daedalus entitled the fictive autobiography of his own mythical paragon.[8] His books carried the idea of labyrinth building to the entire world.

In continental Europe in the meantime, there quietly developed a, let us say, advanced historical "labyrinthology." Its visible result came to public view in the summer of 1981. The Munich

Michael Ayrton, Arkville Maze, New York State, with ten-foot-high brick
walls and bronze sculptures of the Minotaur as well as Daedalus and Icarus
in the center. Courtesy of the Armand G. Erpf Fund, New York City.
Used by permission of Georg Gerster, Zumikon-Zürich.

jurist and art expert Hermann Kern organized, in the Palazzo della
Permanente in Milan, an exhibit that attracted wide attention,
whose catalog he worked up into the most comprehensive docu-
mentation thus far existing on the primordial image of the labyrinth: *Labyrinthe—Erscheinungsformen und Deutungen: 5000
Jahre Gegenwart eines Urbilds* (Labyrinths—Forms and Interpretations: The Five-Thousand-Year Presence of a Primordial Image).[9]
This successful exhibition was to be presented in a significantly
enlarged form in Germany, however, its knowledgeable and inno-
vative creator and promoter was overtaken in 1984 by a fatal can-

cer. Hermann Kern left behind, in addition to the Milan exhibits, a voluminous labyrinth archive with approximately thirteen hundred pictures and more than two thousand related publications.

In addition to Hermann Kern's exhibition, there was another in Milan, devoted to artistic expressions on labyrinthine themes in the twentieth century. *Luoghi del silenzio imparziale,* "places of impartial silence," is what the organizer, art historian Achille Bonito Oliva, called the exhibited pictures and objects. Already the previous year Bonito Oliva had made himself the voice of the Italian "transavantgarde" and interpreted the work of art as a labyrinth: "Art in the end returns to that which inwardly moves it and that which its activity is based on; it returns to its real place, the labyrinth, understood as 'work in the interior,' constant delving within the substance of the art of painting."[10] Included among the authors in the exhibition catalog was Professor of Semiotics Umberto Eco, who had recently presented to a stunned public his labyrinthine novel *The Name of the Rose.*[11]

In the year 1981, the hour of the labyrinth also struck in the realm of German literature. Friedrich Dürrenmatt published his autobiographical sketches under the name Stoffe (Matters), of which the first part contained "Dramaturgie des Labyrinths" (Dramaturgy of the Labyrinth), and also the not at all beautiful labyrinth story, "Der Winterkrieg in Tibet" (The Winter War in Tibet).[12]

Three years later Hans Peter Duerr gave us a fascinating glimpse into the archaic origins of the labyrinth in his ethnological adventure book *Sedna oder Die Liebe zum Leben* (Sedna, or The Love of Life), in which he revived to new life interpretations long regarded as obsolete. One is tempted to say that in this book a mysterious cave world is revealed, and that passing through the vulva of the Great Mother, the reader finds the way to the eternally fruitful uterus.[13]

The cave as an existential human symbol altogether seems to have been rediscovered in the 1980s. Hans Blumenberg demonstrated this philosophically in 1989 in his voluminous work *Höhlenausgänge* (Cave Exits). Here too the key word "labyrinth" is not missing.[14]

Introduction

As early as 1987 Manfred Schmeling's work of literary criticism, *Der Labyrinthische Diskurs: Vom Mythos zum Erzählmodell* (The Labyrinthine Discourse: From Myth to Narrative Model), appeared—a penetrating study of the literary formulations of the labyrinth idea, especially in the twentieth century.[15]

After the multiform eruptions of the labyrinthine theme in the 1980s, the insiders were well taken care of. For beginners and semi-advanced students, however, an introductory work is lacking, which deals with both aspects of the labyrinth, the image and the myth.[16]

Thinking people these days have come to have an appreciation of the mandala,[17] which is derived from the culture of India, as an object of reflection and meditation; however, they do not have an adequate idea of the symbol of the labyrinth, which can be regarded as the mandala of the Mediterranean world and of the European culture that arose from it. In Western culture, it is very closely associated with the contents of the ancient saga cycle of the Minotaur in the Labyrinth, with Theseus and Ariadne, and with Daedalus and Icarus. If it hadn't been for this interwoven set of themes, forming a basis for visual and literary expression, the labyrinth probably would have been lost for Europeans as a symbol with vital significance. This is why we have to keep recounting the old stories about the Cretan Labyrinth anew and to see how the idea of the labyrinth has repeatedly cropped up in new stories, from the Middle Ages down to our own times. This is what my book is about; in spite of an approach to the theme that is playful as well as reflective, it is my intention to show the labyrinth as a historical and present reality.

The concept "labyrinth" is not unambiguous, even though it may have seemed so thus far. The person working on a puzzle in the newspaper is working on a *maze*, which offers a multitude of paths to choose from, including paths that go in the wrong direction and turn out to be dead ends. The idea of such a system of false paths is at the root of many of the accounts of labyrinths that have reached us from antiquity. The metaphorical use of labyrinth is also connected with this; it suggests a difficult, confusing situation of which no overview is possible.[18] This traditional, as it were,

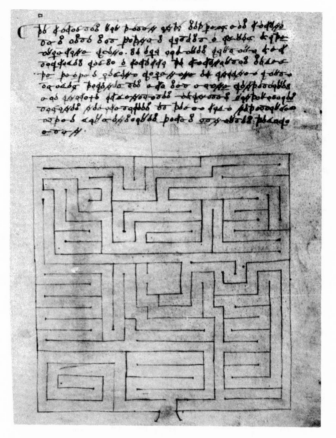

Oldest known representation of a maze.
Giovanni Fontana, Venetian doctor (c. 1395–c. 1455):
Notebook with designs for war machines.

proverbial sense is already to be found in ancient language usages. Gustav René Hocke's book title *Die Welt als Labyrinth* (The World as Labyrinth) alludes primarily to the literary motif of the maze, which did not find pictorial formulation until the fifteenth century.[19]

But in the true sense the labyrinth is not a system of false paths, a maze; up until the beginning of modern times and beyond, it was a geometrical figure showing only a single path and thus containing no possibility of going astray. This classical labyrinth

| Labyrinth with seven convolutions, Cretan type. | Thread of Ariadne as path through the labyrinth. |

can best be understood as an architectural ground plan, a system of lines that represent confining walls, between which the path runs as an unobstructed track. This leads from the only opening in the exterior wall inexorably and choicelessly, with no intersections, to the center and out again, moving back and forth in continual switchbacks in the most circuitous possible fashion in such a way as to completely fill up the interior space. In the most ancient form, designated by Hermann Kern as the Cretan type, the single unmistakable path leads in seven convolutions to the center, the sole dead end. By contrast, in the medieval form, there are eleven convolutions.[20]

The classical labyrinth is not rarely confused with other graphic figures—with spirals, meanders, concentric circles, knots, and woven patterns. Although a strict distinction of the labyrinth from these other forms would make sense methodologically, we have to acknowledge that down through the ages the human imagination has not related with this matter so precisely as that. In fact in the most ancient times when it came to representation of the Labyrinth of Minos on Crete, the preference was to use the meander as an abbreviation for it.[21]

Introduction

That brings us to the mythology surrounding the Minoan Labyrinth. This is a conglomeration of tales and narrative motifs of various kinds and different ages, which have come down to us in ever new variations. Here we find age-old conceptions from Minoan Crete combined with—after being characteristically reinterpreted—Greek sagas and then finally recast in poetic form by Roman authors. Since ancient times, these stories again and again have caught the imagination of the European mind. For some they have been pleasant entertainment, for others, laboriously gained school knowledge; for others still, they have been mysterious communications concerning the origins of our culture, media for the ancient truths, the original knowledge of humankind.[22]

These myths play a key role in the understanding of the labyrinth as symbol. For Europeans, they make the mute geometrical figure speak. They connect it with memories and interpretations that have arisen out of the concrete situations of life.

When the association of the figure with meaningful facts of life is missing, we find ourselves with a mere decoration, maybe a game. A proof of this is provided by the oldest surely datable labyrinth representation. It is a drawing scratched on the back of a small clay tablet found in the palace of Nestor in Pylos. It dates from 1200 B.C. at the latest. The front side of the clay tablet contains a list of the names of ten men, who have brought or received a goat, the record of an administrative procedure that has nothing to do with the labyrinth drawing on the back side. Probably the idea of the labyrinth was already so common that a graffito of it could serve the bookkeeper as an amusing pastime, just a little game.[23]

It is quite another matter with the petroglyph of a labyrinth in the Tomba del Labirinto, a subterranean grave in Luzzanas in Sardinia. This burial site in a stone chamber can in all probability be dated from the third millennium B.C., and if the drawing scratched in the stone can be dated from the same time, it must be the oldest labyrinth representation in existence. Its placement and form connects it with the cult of the dead. It represents the route followed by the dead and at the same time the hope of rebirth, returning out of the womb of Mother Earth. Other such petro-

8

Coin from Knossos, probably 500–431 BC. *Right:* The minotaur
as a dancer in a crouched running posture, leaning on a stick, with tail
and bull mask. *Left:* Squared-off double spirals in a swastika pattern
as a representation of the labyrinth.

glyphs, found in Spain and Cornwall, are presumably connected
with Bronze Age tin mining. In this way the early miners expressed
their vision of themselves in magical terms: they entered the dark
passages of the underworld, the innards of the earth, hoping for a
return to the light of day.[24]

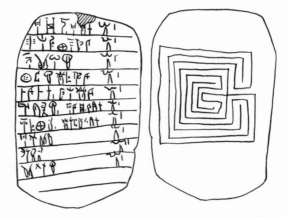

Drawings scratched on a small clay tablet from Pylos, c. 1200 BC.

One of our main concerns is the connection of the classical labyrinth figure with the story of the Cretan Labyrinth. The oldest sure proof of this connection is a scratched drawing found in Pompeii, which was covered by a rain of ash from Vesuvius in A.D. 79. On a pillar in the peristyle of the house of Marcus Lucretius, the archaeologists found a labyrinth of the Cretan type and accompanying it the scratched inscription LABYRINTHUS HIC HABITAT MINOTAURUS—"Labyrinth—here lives the Minotaur." Is this no more than a declaration of learned knowledge, or is it the vengeful act of some naughty boy, who wanted to put out a warning that the owner of the house was some sort of nasty fellow?[27] Whatever the case, the important thing here is the fact that the abstract labyrinth figure is associated with mythical persons and events.

Along with the Minotaur, Theseus and Daedalus are also part of the indispensable dramatis personae of the labyrinth. The meaning of the labyrinth as a symbol has depended essentially, from the time the image was associated with the myth, upon the various ways these "personae" have been understood. As the protagonists in the labyrinth stories of various times, they have been personae in the original ancient sense of the word, that is, masks of persons—images of an understanding of self.

The Minotaur, Theseus, Daedalus—these are images of man,

Introduction

LABYRINTH

Type 1. Labyrinth in the true sense, classical labyrinth

Geometrical figure with round or squared off exterior boundaries, the lines of which are to be understood as confining walls for a path running between them.

Hermann Kern enumerated the following characteristics of the path of a one-path labyrinth *(univiale labirinto)* of this type:

It is without intersections.
It continually switches directions back and forth.
It completely fills up the interior space by running in the most circuitous possible fashion.
It repeatedly leads the visitor past the center he is seeking to reach.
It unavoidably ends up in the center.
It leads back out of the center as the only possible way out.[25]

The oldest surely datable representation of the classical labyrinth is from the thirteenth century B.C. (1200 at the latest), a drawing scratched on the back of a small clay tablet from the palace of Nestor in Pylos.

The classical labyrinth has several variants with different numbers of convolutions and different arrangements of lines. The most important are:

the Cretan type with seven convolutions (see scratched drawing)
the Chartres type: eleven-turn labyrinth with crosslike structure, typical for the church labyrinths of the Middle Ages.

Type 2. The maze, the modern labyrinth

In contrast to the classical labyrinth, this is a system of misleading paths with choices between alternative paths which also contains dead ends.

The maze is the pictorial formulation of the literary motif known since antiquity as the *error inextricabilis,* the errant path whose right direction cannot be found (from Virgil's *Aeneid*).

The oldest representation of the maze labyrinth is to be found in the notebook of the Venetian doctor Giovanni Fontana (c. 1395–c. 1455).

Type 3. The rhizome labyrinth (labyrinth as rhizome or network), the "postmodern" labyrinth

Umberto Eco formulated this third type based on the metaphor of the rhizome suggested by Deleuze and Guattari in 1976. It is a labyrinth of thought, a metaphorical form.[26] On this, see chapter 10.

The Labyrinth

The name of the structure that, according to the saga, Daedalus built for King Minos of Crete, the "prison" of the Minotaur; called the "House of Daedalus" *(domus Daedali).*

11

Petroglyph in the Tomba del Labirintho, Luzzanas, Sardinia.
Diameter c. 30 cm.

the male, a point made not only by our modern feminists. In point of fact, the memory of Ariadne, the original lady of the labyrinth, has practically disappeared in the course of the history of European culture. What has survived in the male story of the Labyrinth is the clue that helped Theseus, the proverbial "thread of Ariadne." Sympathy for the Cretan princess has been expressed almost solely by composers. We find it in Claudio Monteverdi's fragmentary opera *Ariadne's Lament*, and in Richard Strauss's opera *Ariadne on Naxos*, composed at the beginning of this century. At the end of the twentieth century, the moment has certainly come, not only to lament Ariadne, but also to restore to her her ancient rights.

Is the labyrinth a mandala of Western culture? The ambivalence of the symbol seems to speak against this. It is a symbol of the path we have to travel, but this can be a path leading either to well-being or misfortune. It is surely not a symbol that one can

Introduction

Scratched design from Pompeii.

receive into oneself in meditation without disquiet. It is an *open mandala* in a double sense: one opening leads both in and out, in modern times even several. This signifies that there is both an inside and an outside, tension and a dynamic. The labyrinth is also open in the sense that it represents a full range of actual and potential meanings—a hopeless business for dogmatics and perfectionistic encyclopedists! Keeping this in mind, I shall begin my story about the labyrinth. It is my idea to tell a lot—without sparing quotations either—so that the old and new images and stories can come alive and speak.

ONE

The Minotaur

Theseus drags the dead Minotaur out of the Labyrinth.
Central part of a drinking bowl with red figures (440–430 BC).

*It is the Minotaur
who conclusively justifies
the existence of the Labyrinth.*
—JORGE LUIS BORGES

Accommodations had to be prepared for an extraordinarily strange being. Or should I say, a prison had to be built? Or a temple? Yes, it had to be a place for distant veneration and propitiatory sacrifice, but at the same time, a kind of cage and oubliette, so that the inhabitants of the island would be forever safe from its occupant—which had to be withdrawn forever from human sight.

The monstrous miraculous being was born to Minos, the king of Crete, from the womb of his wife Pasiphae. The bullheaded Minotaur was half human, half animal. His name meant the "Bull of Minos," and he was the one and only son of the king. Yet he was not really the king's son but rather the child of Pasiphae's illicit love affair with a wondrous white bull. Or was it perhaps, as it were, a sacred intrigue, divinely intended, of the type that lies beyond the grasp of human notions of morality? There is no doubt, however, that the legendary result of it, the deformed divine spawn, constituted an outrageous scandal for the horned king of the mighty kingdom of Crete, an unparalleled disaster. Nonetheless in itself it was an object of astonishment, of wonder. This is expressed in the Minotaur's other name, Asterius, the "star being," who is represented by Greek vase painters with a body speckled with stars.

In spite of all the advantages that the extraordinary being might have had, for Minos there was no doubt: the unloved bastard had to disappear—quickly and completely. But this was something for which he needed some really good advice. Where to and how with suitable honor?

Fortunately, for a time there had been living in Knossos, the city that was the royal seat, a refugee from Athens, who had been accused of murder in his home city and had managed to slip away on a ship to Crete in the nick of time. Minos had granted him asylum on account of his ingenious technical skills, for which he was already renowned in Athens. Daedalus was his name. Now he could show Minos his gratitude.

There was nothing Daedalus had not invented, especially in the way of tools. Now he was called upon as a master builder. And he fulfilled the task Minos laid upon him with the perfection of which only he was capable. He conceived and built the Labyrinth, an architectural miracle, which fully met the complicated requirements. It was a container for the Minotaur that was a prison, hiding place, and temple at the same time—a far-flung system of convoluted passages that led to the midpoint, the den of the monster. It was made in such a way that the way in was inescapable, and the way out was all but impossible to find. For the outsider, the whole thing was an extremely baffling and confusing affair. Just thinking about it could make one dizzy. For the initiate, by contrast, it fulfilled its purpose with the greatest perfection. It made the Minotaur disappear for all time, for once taken in, he could never find the way out. It also made it possible to purvey to the two-natured thing—half animal, half human—the victims that were his due, human sacrifices that would reach the center of the Labyrinth but could never come out again.

And the Minotaur vanished into it, out of the sight of the unhappy king and the sensation-craving public, perhaps also out of the mind of his mother, who could forget her white bull and once again dedicate herself to her royal mate. The results did not fail. Pasiphae bore other children to her lord in marriage, real children of Minos, among them Androgeos and Ariadne.

Both grew up and attained renown, Androgeos through acts of heroism, which perforce took him off to the mainland, to Attica, where King Aegeus ruled; and Ariadne through the glamour of her appearance—she possessed a starlike radiance that was reminiscent of her half-brother Asterius. She became known as "the utterly pure one" and "the utterly clear and bright."

What Androgeos encountered in Attica cannot be said with

certainty. The most common view on it is that King Aegeus sent him up against the Bull of Marathon, and like many others before him, he was killed by the savage beast. But what does "sent by Aegeus" mean? The expression has the feel of an ex post facto attribution of blame. The challenge of pitting his prowess against the famous bull must have attracted the Cretan prince.

The hideous news of the death of his beloved son nearly killed the Cretan king. He swore to wreak terrible vengeance on King Aegeus and the Athenians. In those days King Minos ruled the Mediterranean with his fleet. He landed on the Attic coast and quickly subdued Athens. Henceforth the Athenians had to provide a dreadful tribute. Every ninth year seven boys and seven girls had to be sent to Crete to be sacrificed to the Minotaur in the Labyrinth.

When Theseus, the son of King Aegeus, defeated the Bull of Marathon, eighteen years had already passed, and lots for the group of victims were having to be drawn for the third time. Theseus, the young daredevil, caught scent of a new adventure and voluntarily presented himself as one of the seven youths (though some say that he too was drawn by lot). In any case, this third time around, he was one of the would-be victims, and that is what counts. The ship bearing the prince and his companions set out for Knossos under a black sail. Since Aegeus had not yet given up all hope, the crew, following his instructions, also carried a white sail in the hold, which was to be hoisted in the case of a fortunate return home. The wily Theseus must have succeeded in arranging a rendezvous with the royal princess Ariadne immediately upon arriving in Knossos. She fell in love with him at first sight and made him swear to take her as his wife if he successfully got out of the Labyrinth. But in order to help him succeed, she gave him a ball of yarn, with the help of which he could mark the way into the Labyrinth and then find his way back out. Theseus swore on everything sacred to marry her and take her back with him to Athens.

And the very same night he set forth on the way to the Minotaur.

He fastened one end of the thread of yarn to the doorpost at

Theseus and Ariadne, on a Cretan pitcher from Arcadia
(early seventh century).

the entrance, as Ariadne had told him to do. Slowly unwinding the ball of yarn, he strode confidently through the darkness of the passages until he found the chamber of the sleeping monster.

How Theseus killed his horrible adversary ultimately remains a secret. Following Ariadne's instructions, he should have grabbed him by the hair of the forehead and sacrificed him to Poseidon. Did he run him through with the sword that Ariadne had thoughtfully provided him with? Did it come to a real duel between equal adversaries, or did Theseus overcome the bull-headed creature in his sleep? Let us assume that it was pretty much a proper chivalric duel, Theseus with a sword or club, the Minotaur with a stone, or both of them wrestling with their hands until the bull-man col-

Theseus fights the Minotaur.
Shield relief from Olympia, c. 600 BC.

lapsed in the Athenian daredevil's stranglehold. At this moment
Theseus became a true hero, the liberator of his companions and
his paternal city.

What followed was almost a child's game: Ariadne's thread,
rewinding the ball of yarn as he went, he found his way out of the
Labyrinth to freedom and to Ariadne's passionate embrace. He
freed his companions from Minos's prison by a ruse. Before board-
ing the ship with them and Ariadne, he staved in the hulls of the
Cretan ships. Now the rescued victims were out of reach of Minos's rage.

A few days later he landed on the isle of Dia, which today is
called Naxos. What happened there is once again so shrouded in
mystery that what has come down to us is only speculations, age-
old, handed-down speculations, which moreover contradict each
other. According to the tale of the ascent to heaven of Ariadne, it
was not granted to Theseus to bring his beloved home, for the god

Dionysus appeared on Naxos, carried off the beautiful bride, and celebrated a sacred marriage with her. Was Ariadne already previously the god's betrothed, and were his actions, as many suspect, only the payback for the disloyalty that had flared up in Ariadne's love for Theseus?

The best known account of what happened on Naxos speaks of Theseus's disloyalty. According to this, he simply forgot the sleeping Ariadne, left her behind on the coast and sailed away. But how could we explain such disloyalty on the part of a great hero? Inveterate male fantasy says: Heroes don't get hung up on details; they pick every flower of love along the way. Theseus's new love was said to be Aegle, "light," a daughter of Panopeus, a maiden of light like Ariadne. Should we attribute such cynicism to Theseus?

No, the apologists say, the hero was put under pressure, either by insistent haranguing on the part of Dionysus, supported by Pallas Athena, or by an intimidating dream sent to Theseus by the love-crazed god. And why, moreover, they say, should Theseus, who to his chagrin had to give up his beloved Ariadne, not have consoled himself with Aegle?

By contrast, the confirmed moralists among the storytellers call down upon the untrue bride Ariadne the cruel revenge of heaven. Either Artemis killed her with her arrows or she died in childbirth on the island, abandoned by everyone. Seen from the standpoint of moralism, she deserved no better. After all, the princess had delivered her half-brother the Minotaur to a stranger's knife, acted against the state in an important matter that symbolized the supremacy of the Minoan kingdom over Athens, and had deceived her father Minos. It was not only treason, it was high treason!

In any case, Theseus left Naxos without his beloved. But he kept a statue of Aphrodite that Ariadne had brought with her from Crete. When he landed with his companions on the isle of Delos, he made an offering to Apollo and set up the statue, which was thereafter venerated by the inhabitants as Ariadne Aphrodite. To celebrate the successful liberation, the hero and the youths and maidens danced a circle dance, which imitated the windings of the Labyrinth in a particular rhythm. From that time on, the inhabitants of Delos danced the *geranos,* the crane dance, at the feast of Ariadne. But the young people who had been saved resumed their journey homeward.

When they were approaching the coast of Attica, in their happiness they forgot to exchange the black sail for the white one. Aegeus, the waiting king, caught sight of the black sail that the ship had been carrying at the time of its departure and threw himself in total despair from the cliffs. Thus Theseus became his successor. But that is not all—from that time forth the Athenians honored him as the founder of their city-state, which arose out of the united communities of Attica, and later on he was regarded by them as the wise ruler who had placed limits on the royal power and started them off on the road to democracy.

It is a sad story, full of human disaster, this story of Minos and Pasiphae, of the Minotaur and the Labyrinth, of the somewhat shady refugee Daedalus, of Theseus and Ariadne—a tale of marriage violation, of uncurbed passion, of lying and deceit, treason and disloyalty, but also of the lure of adventure, of cleverness and courage, of rescue and liberation, and not least of all, of love that makes possible the seemingly impossible. For many centuries it has been retold again and again in new ways and has become inextricably bound up with the millennia-old notion of the labyrinth, this mysterious image of human life in this world.

TWO

The Master Builder

The Labyrinth of Crete.
Drawing by an unknown Paduan miniaturist, c. 1465.

*Minos resolved to banish his shame from the house
and to close it up in a sinister edifice with many chambers. Daedalus created the work with the art of the
most celebrated masters. And he fitted out its chambers with deceptive signs; into the windings of the
muddled tangling passages he misled the eye.*

—OVID, *Metamorphoses*

Theseus did not need Ariadne's thread in order to reach the center
of the Labyrinth but to find the way back out. Isn't that odd?
Shouldn't we presume that the way in and the way out are identical
and that the way out could be found with the same certainty as the
way in? Or were there two different paths, the one harmless but
the other leading in a false direction, so that escape was difficult or
as good as impossible?

André Gide, in his story about Theseus, resolves the problem
of Ariadne's thread in his own original fashion. He presumes that
there is only a single path, yet that for the way out special help
is necessary because Daedalus has accoutered the Labyrinth with
narcotic mists, which cast the visitor into a fascinating dream
world. Caught in the labyrinth of his own fantasies and visions, he
could go back out, but he does not want to. In order to save Theseus from this fate, Ariadne, who is in love with him, gets a thread
from Daedalus that is sufficiently strain-resistant to make a successful outcome of the enterprise possible. What good would con-
quering the Minotaur have done if she had lost her beloved
Theseus in a drug paradise?

> Therefore when we came to the entrance to the Laby-
> rinth—a gate decorated with the double-axe insignia
> found everywhere in Crete—I made Ariadne promise
> not to budge from the spot. She insisted on fastening the

24

end of the thread to my wrist herself, using a knot that she said was a symbol of marriage. Then she held her lips pressed to mine for what seemed like an endless time. I was in a hurry to get on with things.[1]

So much for the modern version!

The unknown Paduan artist who in the middle of the fifteenth century depicted the Minotaur as a centaur also provides a clear solution. There is only one way that leads both in and out. And so that everyone who looked at his work would also note this, he marks the one and identical entrance and exit with the Latin word *via*.[2]

This late medieval miniature gives us a further hint. Whenever someone draws a labyrinth, they are drawing an architectural blueprint. Curiously, however, our imagination fails when it is called upon to construct a building on this plan. Could it be that Daedalus's labyrinth was not an actual structure at all in the conventional sense? But then what could it have been that Daedalus devised and then built?

The poet Homer describes in his *Iliad* the story of the battle of Troy, the device on the shield made for Achilles by the limping god, Hephaestus.

> And upon it the wide-famed Limper
> Depicted a circle dance
> Resembling that, which once in spacious Knossos,
> Daedalus fashioned for braid-adorned Ariadne.[3]

A circle dance for Ariadne? The Greeks called it *choros,* meaning either a dance or the place meant for the performance of the dance. Another hint comes from a Mycenaean clay tablet, founded in Knossos and dated from 1400 BC.[4] The inscription on it can be translated with the following words:

> A honey pot for all gods
> A honey pot for the Lady of the Labyrinth.

Ariadne—the Lady of the Labyrinth—is she now a goddess to whom offerings are made? Is the Labyrinth a cultic site or a place for sacred dancing with passages arranged in a labyrinthine fashion?

The Master Builder

I imagine the following. Daedalus has devised for the divine Ariadne a dancing ground that was at the same time a work of art, and there in her honor the young people, seven youths and seven maidens, dance a circle dance, with Theseus in the forefront, leading the group. Theseus has in his hands the thread of Ariadne, perhaps a rope that binds them all together—and thus, moving back and forth, dancing and singing, they come to the middle of the Labyrinth. But only Theseus really gets there, not his companions, for at the end of the convoluted path, the chain of dancers comes to a standstill. The dance is ended because the leader has come to a dead end, because he is caught in the center of the Labyrinth. For this, the only help is Ariadne's thread. And so they turn around and dance back out, but without the one who has hitherto been the leader, who now is on the end of the chain of dancers and is pulled on the rope by the others. Singing and dancing, they arrive at the exit.

We could imagine the old story of Theseus and his companions in the Cretan Labyrinth as above. On the way home from their journey to Crete, the young people repeat their dance on the isle of Delos in honor of the Lady of the Labyrinth, Ariadne Aphrodite, the consort of Dionysus.

But where in this explanation is the Minotaur, who is also called Asterius?

Clearly the Greeks associated another traditional story with the story of the journey to Crete of the young Athenians—a myth that has to do with Minos, Pasiphae, and the Bull of Minos. This myth has nothing to do with the dancing ground of Ariadne, but rather recalls age-old Cretan stories of the gods, of sacred caves, of descent into the underworld, and resurrection to new life. And in these stories the divine beast of the early Mediterranean cultures cannot be missing—the bull and his cow.[5]

So what did Daedalus build for Minos and his bull?

The flat dancing ground, the labyrinthine pattern of which was perhaps not built up into walls but just marked by flagstones, becomes in the Greek tales the Labyrinth, a masterpiece of a building, which we conceive of as a cavernous edifice recalling the underworld. But no such thing was to be found on Crete, which had already been announced with regret by the writers of antiquity, and therefore in more recent times the palace of Knossos has been identified with the Labyrinth as the supposed "house of the double axe *(labrys),* a speculation—introduced to the world by the archaeologist Sir Arthur Evans—that is still occasionally passed off as a fact today, despite the existence of better knowledge.[6] A similar fancy, but one that can boast of a millennial patina, is the story of the Egyptian labyrinth. The first account of this stems from the fifth century B.C. The Greek historian Herodotus of Halicarnassus gives an eye-witness report in his *Histories* of the extraordinarily large temple of the dead, which the pharaoh Amenemhet III had built near his pyramid around the year 1800 BC, and he refers to this edifice, which formerly was considered a wonder of the world, as a labyrinth. Now it should be known that this meant nothing more at that time than a large, highly impressive complex of buildings built at great pains out of stone.[7] Half a millennium later the Romans were ostensibly given more detailed information in the *Natural History* of the writer Gaius Plinius (Pliny) Secundus the Elder:

> I shall also speak of labyrinths, the most venturesome of all works of the human hand, which are not just for that reason, as might be believed, mere mental inventions. One still exists in Egypt, in Nomos of Heracleopolis, and indeed the first, as is said, built three thousand six hundred years ago by King Petesuchus, who was also called Tithoes. . . . Daedalus doubtless took this labyrinth as the model for the one he built in Crete, which, however, is only a hundredth the size and contains a multitude of crooked passages, counterpassages, and undisentangleable windings, but which is not such a one as we see on stone floors or children's playgrounds, which in a small area contain a space of a thousand steps that have to be gone round; rather it had a great number of doors put into it to make encounter more difficult and to mislead one back into the errant pas-

sages. After the Egyptian one, this was the second labyrinth; the third was in Lemnos, the fourth in Italy.[8]

The admirable edifice of the pharaoh became, through a process of hearsay, a maze building, the supposed model for the Minoan Labyrinth. The imagination of the myth maker, whose starting point was the Minotaur, shaped men's ideas using the stamp of reality—and not here for the first time! Surely Pliny was an avid reader of the two epic works that became classics of Roman, and then of European literature: Virgil's *Aeneid,* and Ovid's *Metamorphoses.* In the fifth book of the *Aeneid,* he could have found the poetic interpretation of the Troy game played by Roman boys, which could have become the pattern for his own ideas:

> As the Labyrinth on the heights of Crete in ancient times
> Proffered warp and weft of walls full of night and deceptive
>   trickery
> With a thousand seesawing passages,
> Where the meaning of way signs was ransacked
> By a tangle of false paths denying the way back—
> In this way the sons of Troy wove their tracks in a round,
> Giving out retreat and charge as one
> As they played like dolphins
> Who in swimming, nimble in their play,
> Shear through the sea waters
> Of the Libyan or Carpathian Seas.[9]

Finally in the sixth book Virgil brings the Labyrinth to life using the figures of the myth:

> Here was seen the Labyrinth's web
> In which the path was inextricably snarled.
> Yet on Ariadne's great love
> Daedalus took pity; thus himself
> He solved the structure's tangled puzzle paths
> And led the blind step on the yarn.[10]

Hic labor ille domus et inextricabilis error. . . . What stuck in the memory of contemporaries and those who came later was the formula *inextricabilis error,* the inextricably misleading path. It was easy to find the corresponding phrase in Ovid's *Metamorphoses: Et lumina flexu ducit in errorem variarum ambaqe viarum,* "and misled the eye with crooked, convoluted passages."[11] There's no doubt: only Ariadne's thread could have saved Theseus from this deadly tangle and only the ingenious builder of that sinister building could have come up with the saving idea—Daedalus, who felt compassion for the amorous princess.

It is curious that Daedalus's Labyrinth, though conceived as a maze building, was represented for centuries by the figure of the classical one-path labyrinth. Pliny, as his depiction shows, was familiar with the Roman mosaic labyrinth, which drew children into playful movements. And probably it was a child who scratched the labyrinth figure on the house of Marcus Lucretius in Pompeii, along with the commentary *Labyrinthus hic habitat Minotaurus* (see page 13). And what was considered valid in antiquity was also taken for granted in the Middle Ages. It is precisely as though, in the face of all knowledge about the inextricably misleading paths, the triumph of Ariadne's thread as the saving grace had to be celebrated.[12]

We, too, cling to this basic form of the labyrinth, the geometrical form and scheme of movement that for us is a symbol, an idea that is associated in our memory with characters and stories that speak to us of life, of mysterious, horrific, and magnificent life.

As a symbol of all this, it has remained a fascinating sign for people since olden times and can be encountered in the countries surrounding the Mediterranean and beyond, as a petroglyph, graffito, as a floor mosaic, in precious manuscripts, in early printed works, in medieval cathedrals, in paintings and pieces of jewelry, as lawn mazes in England, as "Trojan castles" in northern Europe, and finally as garden labyrinths and mazes, a place for feasting and playing.

In the course of the centuries, notions of the labyrinth have changed in meaning and form. The labyrinth is an idea that fascinates people in ever-new variations. In Europe it has remained bound up in a special way with the name and symbolic figure of Daedalus.

The Europeans later named the Labyrinth *domus Daedali,*

Labyrinth from the east wing of the Roman thermal baths of Verdes
(Blois, France), c. AD 200–250.

maison (de) Dédalus, Haus des Daidalos, house of Daedalus, or,
like the French, simply *Dédalus.* Master Daedalus, the admirable
jack-of-all-trades, became the primal image of the artisan, techni-
cian, and architect, someone with whom a person could be proud
to be compared. The master builders of the medieval cathedrals,
those impressive edifices, reminded us of their specialized knowledge and ingenious achievement by immortalizing themselves in
the labyrinths found in these churches or in keystones adorned
with the sign of the labyrinth. See here, a new house of Daedalus!

And Daedalus built not only temples and palaces, cathedrals
and castles, but whole cities: Troy and Constantinople, Jericho and
Jerusalem—symbolic cities, conceived of as labyrinths—the city as

a protected sacred precinct and as representation of the world, the labyrinth seen as a fortified city with walls, battlements, corner turrets, and a gate at the entrance.

The English lawn mazes still recall this symbol of the city. "Walls of Troy" they were sometimes called. And they recall Daedalus, the inventor of the labyrinthine, winding walls.

THREE

Misunderstandings

Liber floridus by Lambert of Saint-Omer.
Genter Manuscript (c. 1060–1123), fifteenth-century exemplar.

As facing image on the other gate
Was depicted the isle of Crete, rising from the seas,
And Pasiphae, in dire rut,
Secretly in intercourse with the bull,
And the Minotaur, a figure half man and half beast,
Mongrel monument to that polluted lust.

        —VIRGIL, *Aeneid*

Medieval scholarship drew its knowledge from the ancient sources. Lovingly, clever monks and hierarchs gathered the ancient treasures and conveyed them along with their pedagogical zeal to a knowledge-hungry audience—clerics and nuns and, later, students in the universities. One of the most successful anthologies of selected readings of this period was the *Liber floridus,* completed in 1121, by Lambert, a canon in the chapter of the Cathedral of Saint-Omer. This book was distributed in numerous manuscripts up until the end of the Middle Ages; in today's terms, it was truly a best-seller. What could educated people of the time learn from it about the Cretan Labyrinth, the House of Daedalus?

A copy from the fifteenth century shows the figure of the Minotaur in a labyrinth with eleven convolutions.[1] He is a bull with the torso and head of a man, of course finished off with horns, which could belong to a goat as well as a bull—a weapon-bearing hybrid, but still quite handsome to look at. Accompanying the figure are the remarks of the medieval commentator: *Domus Dedali in qua minotaurum Minos rex posuit* (The house of Daedalus in which King Minos shut up the Minotaur); *Dedalus artifex* (Daedalus, the master artisan); *Ycarus filius eius* (Icarus, his son). In the twelfth-century original, we read in addition: *Pasiphe regina* (Queen Pasiphae); and *Minotaurus in laberintho* (the Minotaur in the Labyrinth).

From this list of personae the pious scholars who created and copied out the *Liber floridus* omitted the famous pair of lovers of the ancient story: Theseus, the royal prince of Athens, and Ariadne, the daughter of Minos and Pasiphae. Theseus is only mentioned in passing in the précis of the story that takes up the bottom part of the page. Ariadne, the most radiant figure in the whole story, appears nowhere on the page. The Cretan princess and her thread obviously did not suit these scholars' notion of the tale. Lambert of Saint-Omer was interested in curiosities and wonders of the world, especially of the architectural variety, and for him, these wonders included the Labyrinth of Crete, which he conceived of as a combination of a cave and a house. Naturally in the presentation of this wonder its inventor and builder had to be given his due. What prompted him to build his abominable cave house, and what were the consequences of this for him and his son?

Let us attempt to translate the Latin text of the Labyrinth story:

> Pasiphae, the queen of the Cretans, had sex with a bull, and she did it by slipping into a wooden cow, which had been ingeniously made for her by Daedalus. And in this way she became pregnant and bore the Minotaur, half man, half bull. When it was born, on the king's command Daedalus built a cavelike structure called the Labyrinth, and over it, a house. And the Minotaur was put into it. When Minos, the Cretan king, had defeated the Athenians in battle, he imposed the following tribute upon them: At the end of every three years, they must send twice seven young men to feed the Minotaur. King Minos was full of wrath against Daedalus, because his gift for innovation had made it possible for the bull to mate with Queen Pasiphae, but also because, through his betrayal, Theseus had been able to kill the Minotaur. . . .[2]

Pasiphae's perverse liaison with the bull is immediately mentioned twice, a miracle of a quite peculiar nature. Shaking our heads, we take it in.

In the stories the Greeks told about this, we learn somewhat more about this strange love of the queen's. Pasiphae was not just anybody, but the daughter of the sun god Helios and moon goddess Perseis. She is "the all-illuminating one." Of all people, this top-drawer divine being fell in love with a bull, and of course not just an ordinary one, but a wonderfully beautiful, radiant white one, which the gods had sent to Crete.

It is told that King Minos turned to the god Poseidon for confirmation of his rule. He asked him for a sign, for a sacrificial animal with which he could make offering to the god. At this moment, the radiant white bull swam up on shore, and Minos was so fascinated by his having appeared in this way that he kept him for himself and killed another animal in his place. Poseidon's revenge did not fail. He caused the queen to burn with passionate love for the divine bull, a particularly severe punishment for a self-important man like Minos. This passion, which was not only illicit because it was a violation of marriage, but also unnatural and morbid, would have driven Pasiphae relentlessly to her end had it not been for the confidant of the royal family, the clever Daedalus, who came up with a satisfactory solution for the problem. He constructed a wooden frame, which he artfully covered with a cow hide, and had the queen climb in. The ploy did not fail. The divine bull was deceived and excitedly mounted the dummy with the tender inner life. It is not hard to imagine the laughter of the Greeks when they heard this story from ancient Crete, nor the pious indignation of the clerics and nuns who read the *Liber floridus* either. In both cases, they would have felt a sense of moral superiority comparing themselves to the ancient barbarians, and this would, only with difficulty, have blotted out a sense of cultural dependency on them. For the ancient Cretans were in many respects superior to the ancient Greeks who finally conquered them, and the same is true of the ancient world in relation to the Christianized Europeans. Daedalus the artist and master builder, whom the Athenians later reclaimed, was the very epitome of Crete's cultural superiority over its conquerors.

Following the traces of age-old memories preserved in the myths, let us go back a few centuries and more before the Homeric period in Greece to Minos's island kingdom.[3]

The Greeks were not only aware of Pasiphae's divine origin,

Genealogy

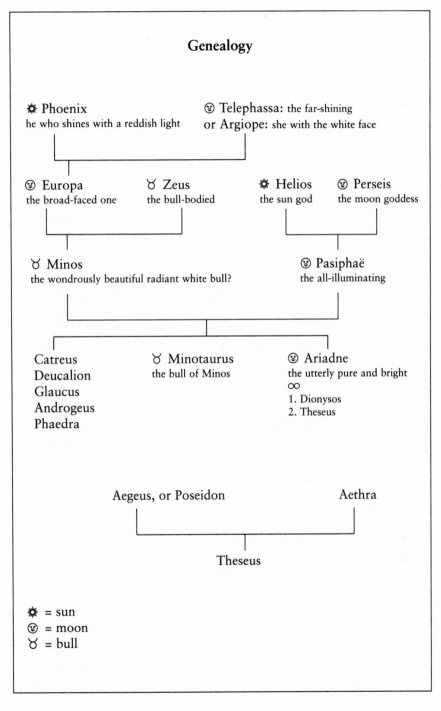

☀ Phoenix
he who shines with a reddish light

☽ Telephassa: the far-shining
or Argiope: she with the white face

☽ Europa
the broad-faced one

♉ Zeus
the bull-bodied

☀ Helios
the sun god

☽ Perseis
the moon goddess

♉ Minos
the wondrously beautiful radiant white bull?

☽ Pasiphaë
the all-illuminating

Catreus
Deucalion
Glaucus
Androgeus
Phaedra

♉ Minotaurus
the bull of Minos

☽ Ariadne
the utterly pure and bright
∞
1. Dionysos
2. Theseus

Aegeus, or Poseidon

Aethra

Theseus

☀ = sun
☽ = moon
♉ = bull

but also knew who King Minos's parents were. His father was the celestial god Zeus, who had freed the beautiful Europa.[4] Europa was described as "with wide eyes" or "with broad face." She was the daughter of King Phoenix, from whom Phoenicia got its name. The word *phoinix* signifies the reddish color of the sun. Europa's mother was Telephassa, "the far-shining," or Argiope, "she with the white face." Mother and daughter thus resembled the face of the moon. One day Zeus caught a glimpse of Europa plucking flowers on the sea strand and fell in love with her. He came to her in the form of a bull, not an ordinary one, but a tricolored bull, as is depicted on an old vase. According to the poets, the bull's breath had the fragrance of crocus. Europa was so taken with his appearance that she willingly seated herself on his back and let herself be carried over the sea to Crete. There the celestial god made love to her in a cave on Mount Dicte; or, as others have it, near the city of Gortyn in the boughs of an evergreen plane tree—in this case more likely in the form of an eagle than that of a bull. Some also say that the real god mate of Europa was King Asterius, the star king. But isn't it precisely Zeus, the father of heaven, who is the real Asterius?

The sun, moon, and stars seem to have made a date with each other in the Cretan royal family. Shouldn't Minos, the son of Zeus in the form of a bull, have been a bull himself, and in accordance with his origin, a *radiant white bull?* And why shouldn't Pasiphae, *the all-illuminating,* have given herself as the divine cow in passionate love to her husband? Then the Minotaur would have been nothing else than the child of their love, the royal prince and Minos-bull, a new Asterius. In that case the whole story of Pasiphae's illicit love would be nothing more than a big misunderstanding.

But to understand the story completely, we have to delve still deeper into the past. Thus we shall leave these heavenly figures behind and descend once more to earth, to the homeland of the Princess Europa, daughter of King Phoenix. This is the Asian mainland, where the Great Mother was venerated—*natura naturans,* the embodiment of the eternally constant primordial force of nature, the source or ground of life, to which whatever has arisen and

Zeus carries off Europa. Water jar from Caere, sixth century BC.

grown to maturity must return in order to renew itself.[5] There, Europa was not a celestial goddess but one of the many manifestations of the Magna Mater, Mother Earth.

We Europeans have to muster the entire force of our imagination in order to get beyond the patriarchally shaped way of seeing things that is second-nature to us. In the Mediterranean region at that time, there existed a feminine, maternal culture. It was not a male god who ruled the world, but the Great Goddess, the mother of all life. She remained ever the same, while her *paredros,* so to speak, her constant companion, her beloved in the form of a bull, was subject to the change of seasons and thus died and was resurrected.

In order for new life to arise from the Great Mother annually, the bull-man, the embodiment of fertility, had to carry out a *hierosgamos,* a sacred marriage, in the cave-womb of the goddess and thus rejuvenate himself.[6] The return to the womb of the mother for sacred cohabitation is simultaneously lethal and life-renewing. The begetting of new life has the death of the old form as a prerequisite; the beloved becomes the son, and the son becomes the new beloved. A bizarre conception! Stranger still is the idea of killing the beloved: the bride-mother tears her bull-shaped *paredros* to pieces, and this makes it possible for his seed and blood to arise as the new vegetation. The same happens, according to some accounts, to the god Dionysus, who in the form of a bull is annually torn to pieces by the Bacchantes, only to be reborn in the spring.[7]

Minoan Crete also took part in this cultic tradition in the earliest times. In accordance with this, Pasiphae, the cow goddess, would have had to be relocated from heaven to earth and become a mother goddess like Europa; and Minos would have been her bull-bodied *paredros,* who every year, or every nine years in the Great Year, would die a sacred death for the sake of regenerating nature and kingdom. Death and birth took place in the womb of the goddess, the mother-lover, deep inside the cavern-labyrinth, represented perhaps by priestesses and priests, who—identified as cow and bull by the use of masks—carried out the ritual *hieros-gamos.* We might also well suppose that a bull was killed as the representative of the son-lover of the goddess.

In the imagination of the Indo-European conquerors of Crete, who simply did not understand these cultic activities, the ritually celebrated sacred marriage would have become a tragicomic sex-and-crime story[8] connected with the hero saga of Theseus.

The key point in the misunderstanding was the Minos-bull figure, whose name in classical times was still Minos Tauros. From one bull, three different beings developed: King Minos, who lost his bull-like qualities; the white bull of Poseidon; and the bull-man who was shut up in Daedalus's Labyrinth. The *paredros* of the divine Pasiphae, the son of the sacred cow, became in the imagination of the Greeks the hideous monster who devoured the Greek hostages and could only be subjugated by a princely hero from Athens.

Prejudices rule the world, even when an acknowledged reality speaks against them. Thus it went with the Greeks. In their myths, Minos was the wise law-giver, who every nine years, in the Great Year, sought out the cave of Cretan Zeus in order to carry on confidential conversations with his father, which enabled him to rule wisely for another nine years. From this arose the tale of the birth of Zeus in the cave on Mount Dicte, just where the father of heaven, in the form of a bull, cohabited with the divine mother

Pasiphae and her son. Interior of an Etruscan bowl, 340–320 BC.

Europa.[9] And why should it be precisely every Great Year, that is, every nine years, that Athenian hostages were brought to Crete as tribute? The *Liber floridus* still recalls this when it says, *semper post tres annos,* and really means *every Great Year.* The insight of the Greek intellectuals failed them despite these very clear indications; otherwise they would have been able to track down the secret meaning of these old stories. We, the children of the enlightened twentieth century, are able to see through to the heart of the old myths, thanks to the productive imagination of our scholars.

Now as far as Daedalus is concerned, the Greeks, misled by the Athenians, believed that he was really one of theirs, whom fate had cast up on the isle of Crete. There he not only fashioned the

41

Seal ring from Mycenos, c. 1500 BC.

cow getup for Pasiphae and the Labyrinth for the Minotaur, but also made possible the conquest of the Athenian hero Theseus over the Cretan monster by providing Princess Ariadne with the famous ball of yarn. The *Liber floridus* reflects this in the words *quia suo indicio Theseus Minotaurum occiderat,* "because through his betrayal Theseus killed the Minotaur." Fundamentally speaking, Daedalus was to blame for everything, but it should be clearly noted that, as posterity saw it, he was an Athenian, and the later Europeans were still very proud of this.

Mistakes make history what it is. Where would European art and literature have been without these fruitful misunderstandings?

FOUR

Liberation

Tantric diagram from India, c. eighteenth century.
The convolutions recall the windings of the intestines.
The way forks at the entrance, a deviation from the usual conception.

My life is the hesitation before birth.
—FRANZ KAFKA, *Diary* (January 24, 1922)

What the Minotaur was all about was actually a matter of contro-
versy from the very beginning. Convinced Athenians, for whom
love of the fatherland was the highest virtue, held strictly to the
view reduced by Euripides to this concise formula: "a mongrel
being, an evil freak."[1] An evil freak is something that can be killed;
a monster that devoured Athenian youths was something that had
to be exterminated! For these patriots, any other point of view
constituted a weakening of the national myth, an indirect deroga-
tion of their hero Theseus, their savior, and the founder of the
Athenian city-state. Unfortunately this defamatory view has ended
up being adopted without reserve by the European tradition! The
Cretans defended themselves to no avail against the Athenian pro-
paganda. According to Philochoros, presumably a leftist intellectual, they claimed that "the Labyrinth was nothing more than a
prison, which had nothing evil about it beyond the fact that the
prisoners could not escape; and Minos instituted a tournament of
arms, offering as a prize to the winner the children who were kept
in safekeeping in the Labyrinth for just that length of time."[2] The
Labyrinth nothing more than a state prison?! If the Cretans did not
deny the existence of the Minotaur outright, they at least con-
tended that he did not kill and eat people.

   If we are going to be honest, we have to confess that it's not
really possible to come up with anything sure and definite concerning the Minos-bull. But for all that, I see no reason to go along
with the prevailing prejudices, no matter how productive it may
have been for literature and art. I don't see why we should be
sucked in by this point of view without at least a look around. My
suggestion? Let's read the story of the Labyrinth against the grain.
We won't for the moment let Theseus into the picture. Instead, by

44

Liberation

Hopi: Tápu'at (Mother and Child).   Hopi symbol of Mother Earth.

way of experiment, we'll take the side of the ancient Cretans and take the Minotaur as a hero.

Now the Labyrinth, that most enigmatic of all places, is a prison and a sheltering, protective cave at the same time—an interior space that opens to the external world but also shuts it out. In it is the Minotaur, who is called Asterius, a hybrid of human and animal.

The first sentence of our story could be: In the middle of the Labyrinth, the Minotaur was sleeping.

I imagine the following: There lies a being asleep who is equal parts animal and human, but who at some point is to become entirely human. Dark is the cave and narrow the convoluted passage through which the young creature must find his way in order to behold the light of the world. At the end of it, he will come out in the open, be born into freedom.

The Labyrinth: a uterus drawn out long, seven times convoluted, like the loops of the intestine. In much this way did people before the Enlightenment conceive of the birth canal. The fantasies of early childhood coincide here with the intuitions of age-old myths, with anatomical doctrines of the Middle Ages and magical notions concerning birth in India.[3] Among the Hopi Indians today the labyrinth is still a symbol of Mother Earth as well as of birth and rebirth from her.[4] For the pregnant woman, childbirth is often a difficult and painful procedure that requires help both before and during the process. The child must find its way out of the labyrinth of the uterus; it must be guided along the pathway to birth through seven spaces in the innards of the mother. Only when this has been successfully done is a speedy and relatively painless delivery to be expected. How this is achieved can be seen from a book of ritual from India. The gist of what we find there is as follows: "Rub on saffron and water from the Ganges, and draw the labyrinth on a bronze dish; wash this off with Ganges water and give that to the woman in labor to drink; then the birth will come soon, and the birth pains will be calmed."[5] The mother ingests the magically potent labyrinth with the saffron water from the sacred Ganges. Expressed in modern terms, via this channel the child is supplied with the information it needs concerning the pathway to birth; at the same time the pregnant woman receives with the Ganges water a birth-hastening medicament, a laxative, as it were, for in this archaic vision, the bodily orifices are curiously confounded or merged into one.

But modern and enlightened people that we are, we know better: The birth canal is in reality short and straight; the labyrinthine, convoluted windings are the product of childish fantasy. Holy water, whether from the Ganges or a Christian source, is at best a psychological remedy that works on pious, unenlightened souls. All the same, the labyrinth remains today a meaningful symbol of birth, not of the physical process but of psychic birth, the spiritual entry into the world, a symbol of emancipation and self-realization. Mothers, fathers, and other educators should therefore keep the labyrinth in mind as a reminder and object of contemplation, so they will be able to help young people at the right moment deliver themselves from themselves and bring themselves into the world intact. For the hybrid being that wants to become a human being, the labyrinth is an indication of the difficulty of this undertaking and at the same time an affirmation of success, an encouragement to tread the path into open space with confidence.

The beginning. The Minotaur awakens rudely. He is cast out

of the maternal body, driven out of paradise. Painfully he experiences the monstrous aspect of birth: spasms in the womb press upon him, cut off his air and nourishment, drive him into the narrowness of the birth canal and terrifyingly, slowly out of the still comforting darkness and gentle warmth of the maternal womb into the harsh light and cold air of this world.[6] Our first encounter with the world is shocking. There is the parting from the homey familiarity of the inner world of the mother, the tumble into the alienness of the unknown outer world. The cry with which we greet this world amounts to an elemental protest, a still inarticulate curse, for which soon a quite earthy word will fall into place; but at the same time, this cry is a dissonant cheer for being liberated into the open air out of that damned closed-in space—for the optimists, into the anticipated wonder of one's own life. The cutting through of the umbilical cord seals for the time being the adventure of coming into the world.

This experience of the voyage of adventure into outer life is ambivalent, more oppressive than cheerful.[7] When the way back into the lost Garden of Eden is cut off, the only thing that helps is fleeing forward—into uncertainty, into the unavoidable labyrinthine uncertainty of life. The awkward thing about this is that the newborn is by no means made to stand up to the challenges of outer life. More of a pitiful, prematurely and defectively born misfit than a fairy-tale hero setting out to instill fear in the world, it lies there completely helpless, a kind of misplaced little thingamabob, still dazed from the effort of waking up. Were it not for the mother who holds and nurses it, it would be lost. The symbiosis of mother and child, established during the period of prenatal life, continues on and finds its fulfillment in the first days, months, and years of childhood. For the infant, the world is all but completely identical with the warm, soft, smiling mother. Reality is not yet divided into ego and non-ego; it is still a unity called "mama" in which the little one participates. However, the world outside of mama, the non-mother,[8] makes itself increasingly evident, not suddenly, but occasionally, as it were, in fits and starts, in bearable doses. It is not even to be imagined that in the first moment of his earthly life the child could be introduced directly to the terrible and beautiful totality of our earthly life!

The human child has left its mother's womb, the center of the labyrinth, and begun its voyage into the world. It is still very close to its origin, and during the next period, it keeps swinging to and fro—further away, closer—but always returning to this center. Is this in order to draw new strength from it for the long and difficult journey to the outside? Through curiosity and inquisitiveness come knowledge and familiarity with the world and at the same time the development of the ego. For "development" we can also say "unfolding," in this case, initially, a process of unwinding, unwinding out of the umbilical cord, which is nothing other than the thread of Ariadne, as inalienable a part of the Labyrinth as the Minotaur. This two-natured being, the symbol of our early existence, unconsciously makes the thread of Ariadne into a clue, the guideline of its developmental saga. With a dialectical pendulum movement it makes its way first in the direction of the exit leading out into the confusing hither-and-thither of the emotions, then it goes back to assure itself of the cozy hominess of its origin, then strikes out once more into foreign territory, anxiously looking back and immaturely backpedaling, ultimately, however, courageously going forward into the consciousness of freedom. Thus it seems that, following an inner necessity, it reaches the exit and becomes a whole person.

Becoming a whole person, a real person, has always had to do with emancipation, liberation from the minority status of childhood and attainment of the legal independence that characterizes the full citizen—and in our sense, the achievement of spiritual autonomy. This is something that happens stage by stage. At the same time one's ego gains substance, one achieves self-reliance. Liberation from the dependency on early ties, however, goes hand in hand with the taking on of new ties. We develop, unwind our way out of one womb and at the same time wind into a new one. It is departure and entry simultaneously—out of the womb of the mother into the womb of the family, then out of this into the womb of society. Psychologists make a great effort to describe these stages scientifically. According to what they tell us, puberty, the departure from the womb or bosom of the family, leads to adolescence, the maturity of the young adult—presuming nothing comes along to disturb this enterprise and causes it to fail. In any case, integration into the prevailing order and the establishment of a stable ego identity through identification with the values and everything else the society we live in takes for granted, are desirable goals. But is that the same as reaching the exit, attaining autonomy?

After all, it could be that the sense of self-determination experienced within society is to a great extent no more than disguised determination by others. The anonymous pronoun "one" is deceptively articulated as a personal "I." And this "I" reproduces prejudices and preconceptions that are taken for granted as its own understanding. This is an old problem. The first to have articulated it was one who lived and worked in an urban society with democratic traditions—Socrates, in the Athens of the fifth century B.C. In the year 399 B.C., he was sentenced to death and executed by the people's court for allegedly undermining the existing societal order, and particularly, for misleading the youth. Socrates, the son of a midwife, had made it his mission to prepare people for a spiritual birth through a process of incisive questioning. His method is called "maieutic," the art of (intellectual) midwifery.[9]

Plato, a student of Socrates, recounts in the seventh book of *The State* the story of the liberation and preparation of humanity for its true destiny. This is known as the simile of the cave.[10] He puts it into the mouth of his teacher of philosophy, who tells it to Glaucon:

> Imagine people in a subterranean, cavelike room; this has an exit leading up to the daylight, which is as high and wide as the entire cave. They live in this cave from childhood on, shackled at the thighs and neck, so that they remain in place and only look straight ahead; because of their shackles, they are unable to turn their heads.

In contrast to our story, which tells of the dynamic of entering the world, Plato devises an image of rigidified life—people who are incapable of moving look, on the wall of the cave facing them, at shadow pictures, which are produced with the help of a fire behind them. They are permanent patrons of an ancient movie theater who have never had the opportunity to compare the shadow pictures they see with the reality these represent. The chained-up people are pretty well convinced that in these moving pictures they are experiencing the only reality that exists. Glaucon is surprised by what Socrates tells him:

> "That's a strange image you present there, and strange chained-up people," he said.
>
> "They are similar to us," I replied. "For to begin with, do you think these people would ever have been able to see anything of themselves and others beside the shadows that the fire cast on the side of the cave facing them?"
>
> "How could they," he said, "if their whole lives long they are forced to hold their heads immobile?"

They are similar to us. . . . Held fast by outer, and even more by inner compulsions, often enough we fend off demands to free ourselves from our shackles, demands to stand up and change our way of looking at things. But this is not all that happens to the cave dwellers in Plato's simile. They are required by their liberator to set themselves in motion, to leave their shadow theater, and to go out into the daylight.

And how do matters stand for the Minotaur in his parallel situation?

It is difficult for him, almost impossible, without reliable help, strictly on his own—stuck as he is in the common run of opinions and frequently uncritically trusting as he does in his own wishful thinking—to gain a realistic idea of himself and of the world outside him and to learn to act in a way that corresponds with the way things really are.

The Minotaur needs birthing help. That the Labyrinth cannot be dealt with without the help of someone else, of someone loving, intelligent, or even wise is very clearly shown even by the Theseus and Ariadne story as colored by the prejudices of the Athenians. The disobedient daughter of Minos makes it possible for the

Liberation

Athenian prince to find his way out to freedom by furnishing him with the ball of yarn and a sword. Should we just change the story and send to the side of the needy Minotaur a friendly Theseus, recruited by his loving half-sister Ariadne? But that's too good to be true. Let's stick with Socrates, the son of the midwife. He would have to come and provide birthing help by freeing him from his chains and getting him to tread the steep path into the daylight, no matter how laborious that might be. And it is a mighty effort, for the path away from the comfortable seat in front of the shadow pictures up into the light is not only arduous, but initially seems completely absurd: "And when he came out into the light, his eyes were so full of the brilliance that he was able to see absolutely nothing whatever of that which was now described to him as the true reality." But nonetheless, whoever accustoms himself to the brilliance and recognizes the reality in the light will no longer wish to return into the formerly comfortable darkness and make do with illusory images. "He would rather put up with anything but that life," Glaucon says, and so admits Socrates is right.

Despite curiosity and the urge for freedom, we are afraid to be born, to be left out in the bright, harsh light of our hopeless yet so very fascinating world. But we really have no choice. Everybody has to take the chance.

FIVE

Rebirth

Lucca, Cathedral of San Martino. Labyrinth below the western portico
of the cathedral on the north side of the bell tower, vertically situated
bas-relief, in which the pathways are left unworked and the
separating walls are chiseled out (c. 1200). Diameter 50 cm.

*Verily, verily I say unto thee, Except a man be born
of water and of the Spirit, he cannot enter into the
kingdom of God.*

—JOHN 3:5

In the old days when the pious people of the Italian town of Lucca
entered the western portico of their Cathedral of San Martino, they
saw on the wall of the bell tower at eye level the representation of
a small labyrinth, in the middle of which originally a miniature
Minotauromachy—the battle between Theseus and the Minotaur—was depicted. One after the other, they walked up to it and
followed the lines with their fingers, with the result that today they
are somewhat worn away. Whoever could understand the Latin
language—which for a long time was only the learned clerics—
found this explanation immediately to the right of the representation:

HIC QUEM CRETICUS EDIT DEDALUS EST LABERINTHUS
DE QUO NULLUS VADERE QUIVIT QUI FUIT INTUS, NI
THESEUS GRATIS ADRIANE STAMINE IUTUS.

Here is the Labyrinth that Daedalus of Crete built and
which no one can leave who is once inside; only Theseus
achieved this thanks to Ariadne's thread.

A stonemason chiseled this out around the year 1200.[1] Was it just
an entertaining game to follow the lines with the finger, or were
the churchgoers trying to emulate Theseus symbolically before they
entered the space of the cathedral?

It is astonishing that Theseus—as the one who courageously
entered the Labyrinth, conquered the Minotaur, and returned to
the light of the world with the help of Ariadne's thread—was still
a living hero for the people of the Middle Ages.

For the ancient Athenians, Theseus's voyage to Crete was not just another one of adventures, but rather the decisive ordeal before his accession to the kingship, and as I see it, they recounted this tale to their children as a parallel to the adventure of life. They told how the seven boys and seven girls, who expected to meet ruin and death in Knossos, overcame all the dangers through the luck and skill of their royal companion and were given back to their families and city as though reborn. And in the course of time it is possible that another version of this story than the usual one came to prevail, namely, one in which Theseus was picked out just like all the other hostages.[2] King Minos, who came to Athens with his ship, also did not spare the Athenian king's son; together with the others he had to board the foreign ship to be sacrificed in the Labyrinth. But Theseus already began to demonstrate his extraordinary qualities on the voyage over. Minos, who had fallen in love with one of the Athenian girls, took the liberty of touching her cheek as though he had the right to dispose over her as over a slave. She screamed in outrage and called Theseus. Theseus confronted the king and rebuked him: "Son of Zeus, your intentions and thoughts are unfitting! Beware of committing an act of violence!" Self-assuredly, Theseus asserted his equal standing with Minos by naming Poseidon, the god of the sea, his father. Minos, doubting the divine origin of the young man, whom he knew only as the son of Aegeus, demanded proof. Minos himself prayed to his father Zeus to confirm his own filiality by sending a thunderbolt, which in fact came. For Theseus, he devised another form of verification. He tossed a ring into the water and challenged his adversary to fetch it from the sea bottom. If Poseidon was really his father, the god should help him, Minos asserted. Unabashed, Theseus plunged into the depths. Minos, in spite of himself, was impressed by the youth's courage. Nevertheless, he had the ship speed up as though the matter were already decided.

What took place under the waves remained hidden from him and Theseus's companions on board. Dolphins carried Theseus to the house of his father, the palace of the Nereides on the bottom of the sea. There he was crowned by the queen, Amphitrite, with the head garland—woven with roses—that she had received as a wedding gift from the god of love. Wearing this royal adornment, Theseus resurfaced beside the ship and handed the ring back to the terrified Minos. After this successful epic plunge to the bottom of the sea, who could expect the prince to fail in his mission in the underworld of the Labyrinth? When the time came, what happened in the Labyrinth remained just as hidden from those who remained behind as the events at the bottom of the sea. For the second time, Theseus entered a realm which separated him from the rest of humanity, a realm beyond all previous experience and one that held mortal peril for the luckless and unwitting.

What did he find in the center of the Labyrinth?

According to the saga, it was the horrible monster that he had to kill in order not to be killed, that had to be sacrificed so that the Athenian girls and boys wouldn't become his victims—a very simple calculation! Theseus slew the monster—for him a trial of his manhood, which singled him out above all others; and in addition an act of liberation, which would let all Athenians breathe easier and which would receive unreserved applause from the entire enlightened world. But this old familiar solution is a male martial fantasy, which only just becomes tolerable because of the fact that Theseus escaped with his life merely thanks to Ariadne's thread—to the pleasure, let it be noted, of all modern and ancient feminists.

Let's try it another way. What our hero finds in the darkness at the center of the Labyrinth is not just any hybrid of bull and man, but rather the *mixtum compositum*. The ancient Romans called it the *monstrum sacrum*. Possible translations: "sacred freak," "that damned miraculous creature," "that Minotaur, monstrous in good as well as in evil"—in any case, a divine being, entirely suited to the ideas of the ancient world, according to which the heavens of the gods are populated by beings to whose accounts can be credited numerous rapes, murders, patricides, and acts of incest, to say nothing of acts of madness and bestiality. These are beings put together from odd elements and broken pieces belonging to different levels of reality—human, animal, mineral, cosmic.[3]

Could it be that the Minotaur is a masculine relative of the Sphinx, who denied Oedipus entry into the city of Thebes? The Sphinx is a monster. She has the head of a woman, a lion's body, a

Oedipus and the Sphinx. Attic School, 470/460 BC.

dragon's tail, and an eagle's pinions. She is a real conglomeration of disparities.[4] The solution to the riddle that she gave Oedipus is: man. No wonder, because the Minotaur and the Sphinx are representations of the human being, of the mixed creature par excellence. Man created God in his own image: from the highest gods down to their monstrous derivatives.

In the mystic darkness of the Labyrinth, Theseus meets the sacred monster who is named Asterios; he is astonished, numb before this *mysterium tremendum et fascinans,* this terrifying and at the same time fascinating mystery, the revelation of which he experiences with a mixture of fear and devotion, of respect, desire, and terror.[5] Overwhelmed as well as spellbound, he stands there gawking. However, he does not fall to his knees; rather he thinks the situation over. At this time it would be of no use to him to take some lethal weapon and put an end to the bullheaded monster.

I imagine the following: As insight comes concerning the peculiar nature of the being facing him—a realization which transforms him—a laugh of apprehension rises up in him, a laugh that betokens both nearness and distance, assent and protest. "Look at this—man, the monstrous being that I myself am!" As Oedipus guessed the riddle of the Sphinx, so Theseus penetrates the mystery of the Minotaur. It is a triumph of self-knowledge![6]

For Theseus, in any case, it is a victory in every way. He can now without danger turn his back on this terrifying-fascinating reflection of himself and, using the thread of Ariadne, follow the path to the outside, back into the everyday world, but newborn and transformed into a mature adult—and even more, transformed into his father's successor, into a king. For at the end of his Cretan voyage, Theseus is enthroned in Athens. This occurs as an inner consequence of what the prince experienced on his journey, not, as the saga would have us believe, as a result of an unfortunate mischance.

The cultural sciences refer to what has been recounted concerning Theseus as an initiation. Is it the passage of a young person to the adult stage and his acceptance as a full member of the community. In the closed archaic societies of the nature peoples—in tribal societies—this was and is done by taking the young people away from their families and exposing them in the "bush time," under the guidance of a teacher, to a number of ordeals.[7] However, it is not necessary to mount an expedition into the last remaining primeval forests to study this phenomenon. A visit to the opera will do it! What's true for Pamina goes for Tamino too:

> Ein Weib, das Nacht und Tod nicht scheut,
> Is würdig und wird eingeweiht.[8]

> (A woman whom night and death do not frighten
> is worthy and will be initiated.)

These two, however, are initiated into greater mysteries than normal adult existence, a reflection of the fact that there are different varieties of initiation. But wherever and however such a thing takes place, "the novice arises from his ordeal as a completely different being: he becomes someone else."[9] What happens to the initiate is explained in terms of death and reincarnation. It is only the death of the old person that makes possible the birth of the new one. In the folk myths, initiatory death is symbolized by darkness, cosmic night, the maternal womb of the earth, a hut, or the belly of a monster—images of chaos, of primordiality, of the devouring and child-bearing depths.[10]

Theseus must face the abyss of the sea and the labyrinthine underworld before he can become a man and a king. In the depths of the sea he receives his confirmation as the son of a god. Would it be wrong to say that it is only through his courageous plunge into the water that his godly rank is established? And is what he finds in the center of the Labyrinth just himself as a being who has hitherto remained hidden from him—or is it a dimension of his being that was unknown to him, but one the knowledge of which is indispensable for human maturity?

Following the thread of Ariadne, he once more finds his way into the free open air, that is, is successfully resurrected. But this is only the prince who receives the favor of the helpful princess and stands up to the adventure of rebirth. What has happened to the others, his companions on the voyage of initiation? Were they able to participate in the rebirth as well?

Without a doubt, the extraordinary experiences of this journey into expected death makes them grow up. But only Theseus goes the whole way, only he reaches the ultimate goal of the journey. We must immediately add that he does this not only for himself, but as an exemplar, a representative of the others, the son of the king for the whole community. Their participation, however, in the representative initiation is not merely announced, but is symbolically conferred on them on a stopover on the return journey, by means of the crane dance, which recalls Theseus's action in the Labyrinth, ritually enacting it. The exemplary pattern is symbolically repeated.

Even without the Minotaur, the Labyrinth is a model of initiation; and it strikes us as highly probably that the dancing ground of divine Ariadne that Daedalus built can be regarded as a place of initiation for young people.

What could the young people experience when they danced through the figure of the Labyrinth in the ritual of initiation?

An impressive answer to this has been given by Hermann Kern, who developed this experience interpretively out of the unique nature of the figure of the labyrinth.[11] The prospective initiate stands at the single narrow entrance of the Labyrinth. His task is to penetrate into what appears to be the frighteningly complicated inner space, a space that isolates him from those who remain behind as a prison does, through a movement that progressively distances him from those outside, in the same way as if he were dying. The movement through the labyrinthine winding passages requires of him, in addition, a high degree of physical control as well as adaptability. It is an unparalleled challenge. Once he is in the interior, as he dances, he discovers the way to the middle, to the endpoint of the movement, as the longest possible way around. It requires a maximum of commitment, time expenditure, and physical effort. But the novice is also challenged psychologically. The goal is often close enough to reach out and touch, however, time and again he is led away from it. Patience and endurance are indispensable in order finally to reach the center. This, however, is sure to happen, for no false path will cause the venture to fail. Nonetheless, there at the endpoint, he is alone with himself; he experiences self-recognition or encounters something higher. At the same time, the central experience includes a radical change of direction, for only that makes the return possible. A 180-degree about-face means creating the greatest possible distance from one's own past. It is simultaneously the death of the old person and the rebirth of a new one. The way back into the world—almost as hard as the way in—is traveled by a changed person, someone who has found a new form of existence, a new way of being.

Did the pious churchgoers in medieval Lucca think of this or at least intuitively sense it in some way as they followed the lines of the church labyrinth with their fingers?

Whether or not the significance of these primal symbols of life opened itself to him, we do not know. However, a number of

The god Pan—who, like the Minotaur, was made into the Christian
devil—represented as a winged billy goat with occult symbols.
His pipes symbolize the harmony of the seven spheres.

traditions and clues from this period make it clear that the laby-
rinth must have had a new but still comparable meaning for him.[12]
In the meantime, Theseus, the pagan hero, had become part of the
Christian world of ideas with a new name. He was now Jesus
Christ, the god-man who descended into the underworld—
descensus ad inferos—and conquered the infernal monster. The
Minotaur, grotesquely altered, has become the devil, a terrifying

Anastasis: Christ's resurrection or journey to hell.
Fresco in the Paraclesion apse of the Chora Church in Istanbul.

and yet also attractive demon with a human form but goat's or horse's feet, bird's claws, wings, a tail, and horns, who nonetheless occasionally appears in a quite respectable form, resembling an angel, as a well-dressed youth, or as a woman with seductive charms.[13]

The decisive victory over Satan—a fundamental metaphysical decision, thus here also not a brutal annihilation—makes it possible for the new Theseus to liberate the righteous souls imprisoned in Hell and—traveling to heaven—to open Paradise to them.

The labyrinth appears in the medieval interpretation[14] as an image of the world of sin, from the center of which the devil carries out his mischief, even though he has no prospect of long-term success. In theological terms, this means that Christ, by entering death, rising again on the third day, and ascending to heaven, liberated this world from the ground up, along the inner axis of its essential nature, from its dependence on evil, and created a basis for the hope of ultimate and final salvation. Only he was capable of doing this—*thanks to Ariadne's thread,* as the inscription in the Lucca cathedral tells us. This is a somewhat tricky allegory, for if we don't wish to get into theological sidetracks by identifying Ariadne with the earthly mother Mary, Ariadne would not only have to be deified but also made masculine so that the image could fit the Heavenly Father. So we could leave the possible translation at "equipped with Ariadne's thread of divine power."

The observer in Lucca was wisely provided with the help he needed for his interpretation. He only had to turn his gaze to the pillar on the opposite side of the portico to see a representation of the Fall and the paradisiacal tree with the serpent wound about it, grown over with the salvation-bringing root of Jesse, crowned by Christ,[15] another version of what the Christianized labyrinth also means.

These church labyrinths have in common with the Cretan type a single way in and out, without false paths or dead ends. One follows the passage to the only endpoint via the most circuitous possible yet unequivocally efficacious route. But instead of the seven concentrically nested loops that we have had up till now, the figure now gets eleven of them (cf. illustration on page 74). According to Christian number symbolism, eleven stands for sin, trespass, and intemperance (since it exceeds the number of the commandments) and for imperfection (since the perfect number twelve has not yet been reached). It identifies the labyrinth as a world of sin. But the eleven concentric circles have the sign of the Cross laid over them, and this organizes the figure in such a way that the path must turn when it reaches the axes of the Cross and thus makes it into a Way of the Cross. Thus the world of sin is placed under the saving sign of Christ, which conquers Satan. The triumph of the new Theseus over the Minotaurian false paths of the world is all but fully expressed in the unequivocal routing of the classical labyrinth.[16]

Should we conclude that the pious churchgoer not only moved his finger into the center of the labyrinth, but also, with

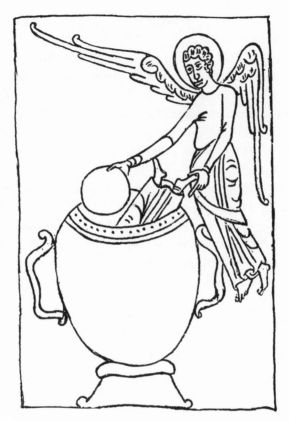

Baptism as Christian bath of immersion.
Illustration from the Roda Bible, eleventh century.

devotion, traced the opposite movement back out of it, in order to symbolically reenact as a baptized Christian the Way of his divine-human Master and demonstrate his willingness to follow his example? Had he perhaps heard the words of Paul concerning initiation?

> Know ye not, that so many of us as were baptized into Jesus Christ were baptized into his death? Therefore we are buried with him by baptism into his death: that like as Christ was raised up from the dead by the glory of the Father, even so we also should walk in newness of life.[17]

Rebirth

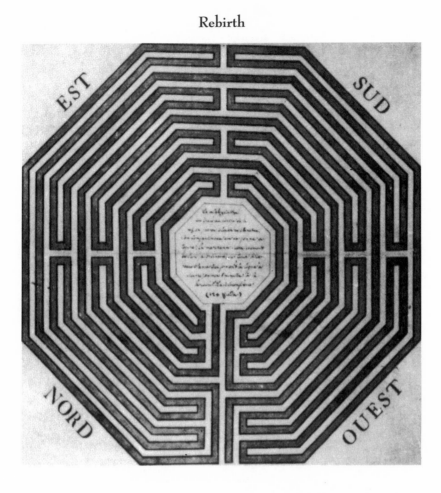

Labyrinth in the cathedral of Amiens, done in 1288 and reconstructed
after the destruction in the years 1827–1897.

In the Cathedral of Amiens and other churches the Christian
symbolism of the labyrinth is heightened by using the form of an
octagon. This, as the octagonal form of many baptistries and bap-
tismal fonts shows, is connected with the Christian initiation of
baptism. It signifies resurrection, perfection, a new beginning.[18]

In case our man in medieval Lucca was not just passing the
time of day with the labyrinth but understood the symbolism and
was taking advantage of it before entering the sacred space and the
sacred activities going on there, he reenacted his baptism ritually;

by this sensorimotor means he consciously repeated in the passages of the labyrinth his initiation into Christendom, which he only knew of from hearsay—another ritual action in which, to the murmur of words in Latin, a splash of water had moistened his head. Born from water and the spirit.

SIX

Concentration

Relief of a labyrinth on a sandstone slab, the sole remains of the cloister
church San Pietro di Conflentu in Pontremoli (near La Spezia), Italy.

Man, attend to the essence, for when the world fails,
Accident disappears, but essence prevails.

—ANGELUS SILESIUS, "Accident and Essence"

In northernmost Tuscany lies the tiny town of Pontremoli, today
an unimportant place on the road from La Spezia to Parma, but in
the Middle Ages an important station of the Via Sancti Petri, the
pilgrimage route to Rome. Of the Romanesque cloister church San
Pietro de Conflentu, today there remains only a sandstone slab
with the relief of a labyrinth on it, the sole vestige of the facade.
We have to assume that the labyrinth was situated in the same
place as in the cathedral of Lucca, under the western portico, vertical on the north wall of the bell tower, for only in that way could
its opening point to the west, as do those of all church labyrinths.

Unlike in Lucca, there is no mention here of Theseus and the
Minotaur, but rather a reference to Jesus Christ as the middle of
the world, indicated by the monogram of Christ IHS in the center
of the labyrinth.[1] The diabolical Minotaur seems to have been
driven out, or perhaps would it be better to say, the Cretan Minotaur has been restored to his rightful position as the son of a god,
product of a sacred marriage between the heavenly father and
Mother Earth, now transposed into Christian terms—conceived by
the Holy Ghost, born of the Virgin Mary? The new Minotaur, too,
had to die in order to bring new life through his resurrection.

On the lower edge of the labyrinth of Pontremoli, we read the
Latin inscription, *sic currite ut comprehendatis,* which recalls the
words of 1 Corinthians 9:24: "Know ye not that they which run in
a race run all, but one receiveth the prize? So run, that ye may
obtain."

Theseus, too, therefore, is tacitly present. Once again it is a
case of a man putting his life at risk in order to win it anew in the
depths of the labyrinth. The way into the interior now becomes a

competition for the victor's prize. The mistakes and temptations of the earthly life, the convolutions of the labyrinth, have become hurdles to be leapt over in order to win the prize of eternal life through Christ, the secret center of this world.

Sic currite ut comprehendatis. A challenge to the monks of the cloister, but also doubtless to the ordinary churchgoers and to the pilgrims on their way to the distant destination of their pilgrimage. Now run, so that you win the victor's prize! That the Christian is a pilgrim on this earth, a *peregrinus,* the meaning of which is tantamount to foreigner or alien, is something that Augustine impressed on Christendom. "You should know that you are pilgrims on the way to the Lord!"

To the extent that one did not pacify oneself by regarding this as no more than a well-meaning pronouncement on the part of this teacher of the Church, because one had found in the oh-so-beautiful world a fixed place of residence,[2] one set about finding ways and means of meeting this lofty challenge. One could do this professionally through the ascetic life of a monk or nun in the solitude of the cloister, or in a more compromised fashion through extraordinary efforts in an otherwise mundane life. One of the most highly regarded means included in this latter approach was a pilgrimage to a near or distant site of grace, on foot or by horse, depending on the degree of penance one had in mind, on one's level of daring, and on one's material resources.

The dream destination for a pilgrimage was the Holy Sepulchre in Jerusalem. But following the bloody conquest of the city in the First Crusade, Jerusalem was only in the possession of the Christians for about a hundred years,[3] and during this time it was almost exclusively adventurous knights or well-to-do merchants who were able, with great difficulty, to enjoy its promised blessings.

Even before the crusades sought to conquer the Holy Land back from the Muslim infidels, papist Rome had already recommended to Christendom Rome as a destination for pilgrimage. To be sure, it couldn't come up with holy sites that were set apart for all time by the life and death of the divine-human Lord, but it had more than enough sites that were distinguished by deeds of the

apostles and martyrs. The veneration of their real and putative remains, their relics, not only brought the city of Rome tremendous
popularity but also an economic boom through the profitable relic
trade, in the service of which innumerable graves along the arterial
roads were indiscriminately plundered. Precious bones of saints for
worship were to be found in the also innumerable churches of the
Holy City. A sine qua non for a successful pilgrimage, however,
was a devotional visit to the seven principal churches, above all, to
the Basilica of St. Peter at the Vatican.

This overabundance of saints was not in everyone's interest.
As we can imagine, in this Roman hubbub of grace and blessings,
it was all too easy to become distracted from the real goal, life-
renewing penance; and so it is no wonder that Peter and Paul soon
encountered some rustic competition, far from urban Rome. This
came in the form of the apostle James, who with his younger
brother John and the later Roman, Peter, constituted the favored
core group of the disciples. The bones of Saint James—Sant'Iago—
were found in a miraculous manner at the beginning of the ninth
century in the northwestern corner of the Iberian Peninsula, which
in the meantime had become Muslim. The place was Compostela,
at the time an insignificant spot in Asturia, which had remained
Christian and in the following period became the center of the
Christian *reconquista*. Santiago de Compostela developed quickly
into the most popular place of pilgrimage of the Middle Ages, particular among the common folk. Its character can be seen in the
fact that the deeply venerated Saint James himself was depicted as
a typical Santiago pilgrim with a conch and a long pilgrim's staff.
Compostela, located on the Western edge of Europe, was for the
Christian peoples of the West a fully adequate alternative to Jerusalem, the unreachable city on the Eastern edge of the Christian
world. One thing both places had in common: both were religious
bulwarks of Christendom against the Muslim menace.

Places of pilgrimage, whether far or near, large or small, were
points of concentration for Christian life, not only places of assembly but also of inner concentration and self-contemplation. An old
song of the Santiago pilgrims makes this clear:

Concentration

Eh'ich die Reise beginne,
Tut es not, dass ich mich
Auf mich selber besinne,
An die Mauer stosse, bis diese fällt
Und mich nicht mehr gefangen hält.
In Zeiten der Sünde
Bin ich gefangen.
Sobald ich mich auf dem Bussweg befinde,
Werde ich Hilfe erlangen.

In a prose translation: "Before I start the journey, I must needs contemplate myself, bang against the wall until it falls away and no longer holds me prisoner. In times of sin I am imprisoned. As soon as I'm on the way of penance, I will have help."[4]

The destination of the way of penance, for most pilgrims, was inconceivably distant; the way of Saint James, *per pedes apostolorum,* was difficult to tread. Uprooted from daily life into an uncertain freedom, the pious pilgrim was exposed to unaccustomed demands and strains—forced companionship with others, mostly foreigners, people different from himself, whose language he did not understand; physical problems and pains, which could put in an appearance quite soon if he walked his feet raw in bad shoes; diseases resulting from weakness or infection, for which no medical help was available; uneasy nights in overfull, primitive inns and hotels, in which often enough he was cheated and robbed; unfamiliar and bad food, a disaster for his stomach. There are accounts of bandits and highwaymen who attacked pilgrims and beat and robbed them; of inns in which women slipped into their beds for money and "out of whorishness";[5] of the drunkenness and debauches of impious pilgrims, of "wenches" who sought to lure the pious into the clutches of the devil—a long list of dangers, temptations, and distractions. If the pilgrim arrived at the holy place of Santiago via the various stations of the way of Saint James, spiritually strengthened by prayer and participation in masses in chapels and churches, then he really did win the victor's prize, not himself exclusively, but along with hundreds and thousands of others—the symbolic concentrate of an entire Christian life!

When he had had his fill of looking at the magnificence of the

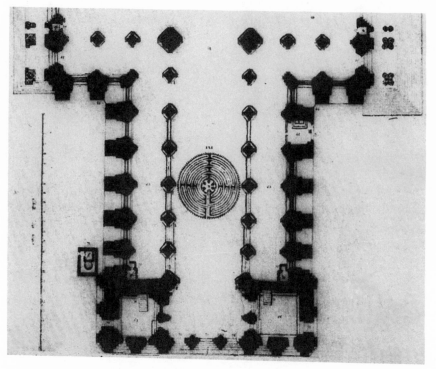

Ground plan of the west facade of the cathedral of Chartres
(from Félibien).

altars and the beauty of the statues of saints, when he had made
his offerings, made his confession, and had been to the table of the
Lord, then he waited patiently in the line of people in front of the
statue of Santiago in order to take leave of it and to kiss it with
profound feeling.[6]

A distance off the roads leading to Santiago—closest to the
Via Turonensis, the "Great Way of Saint James" that started from
Paris, the assembly point, and passed through Tours—lay the Cathedral of Notre Dame de Chartres. There seems to have been a
pilgrimage site on this spot even in pre-Christian times. Legend
recounts that from the earliest times the *virgo paritura* was wor-
shiped there, the virgin who would bear the son of God. Since the
year 876 the church of Chartres has been in possession of a pre-

cious relic, the *sancta camisia,* the holy tunic, which Charles the
Bald presented as a gift from the treasury of his grandfather. According to tradition, it was Mary's garment, which she wore in
labor. Worship of the Virgin Mary, the Mother of God and Queen
of Heaven, took a tremendous upswing after the turn of the millennium and reached a momentary peak at the time of the great
French cathedrals. The sacred relic of Mary soon attracted thousands of pilgrims to Chartres. In the year 1194 the Romanesque
church was largely destroyed by fire, and in the next decades the
marvelous Gothic cathedral was erected, joined to the surviving
west facade with its Royal Portal.[7]

The pilgrim who entered the cathedral through the Royal
Portal and walked a short distance in the direction of the main
altar found himself at the entrance to a large labyrinth on the
floor.[8] Starting from the west, from the direction of the setting sun,
the place of death, he walked through the labyrinth's winding
pathways, moving back and forth pendulumwise, nearing the center and then getting further away again. At the end, with certainty,
he reached the center, here in the form of a six-petaled flower. Was
the reason the whole labyrinth set up at Chartres ended up being
called *la lieue,* "the league," that the way to the center seemed so
long to people? This arduous path to a desired goal was regarded
as similar to a pilgrimage to the Holy Land, and in their imagination people saw before them the holy city of Jerusalem with the
Lord's Sepulchre. For the same reason, the ambulatory labyrinth
in the cathedral of Notre Dame de Reims was called *chemin de
Jèrusalem,* "the Jerusalem road."[9]

Going through a labyrinth seemed like a symbolic pilgrimage
to Jerusalem, the then unreachable goal of the Christian pilgrim's
journey, but at the same time it seemed to bring an inner realization
of the meaning that the actual pilgrimage in this marvelously built
cathedral, lit mysteriously by the colorful glow of its windows,
possessed in the here and now: arrival at what was, in terms of
salvational history, the midpoint of the world, the earthly and
heavenly Jerusalem, as a representation of which the cathedral was
constructed. Did the mysterious words of Revelation sound in the
ears of the pilgrim?

Labyrinth of the cathedral of Chartres (thirteenth century). The pathways
of this ambulatory labyrinth—eleven concentric circles—are 34 cm wide
and as gray as the stone floor around the labyrinth; they are
separated from each other by black-blue strips of marble.
Diameter 12.6 m (west-east) and 12.3 (north-south).
Total length of pathways 294 m.

And I, John, saw the holy city, new Jerusalem, coming
down from God out of heaven, prepared as a bride
adorned for her husband. And I heard a great voice out
of heaven saying, Behold, the tabernacle of God is with
men, and he will dwell with them, and they shall be his
people, and God himself shall be with them, and be their
God.[10]

The flower-shaped center of the ambulatory labyrinth of
Chartres seemed to the meditating pilgrim at once like a representation of the western rose window, which he could see, glowing in
dark colors, by turning around. In its center Christ was enthroned
as the judge of the world, showing his five bleeding wounds.

Labyrinth of the cathedral of Reims.
Pen drawing by Jacques Cellier (c. 1550–c. 1629)

And when the pilgrim left the labyrinth and went further into the main nave, his divine Lord also met him in the colorful radiance of the two other rose windows—in the north as a child with his mother Mary, in the south as the One described in the Book of Revelations, "he that sat upon the throne (and) said, Behold, I make all things new. . . . I am Alpha and Omega, the beginning and the end. I will give him that is athirst of the fountain of the water of life freely."[11]

If the pilgrim's journey is the realistic symbol of the earthly pilgrimage of the Christian to his final home in the glory of the heavenly Jerusalem, then the Church labyrinth is a further reflection of this complex of meaning in the medium of art and ritual. It represents the life-orienting ideas of initiation and rebirth, of pen-

Chartres: modified copy of the west rose window from the Book of
Church Masonry of Villard de Honnecourt (c. 1235), on the same
page as the copy of the labyrinth. The center of the labyrinth
can be regarded as a stylized version of the rose window.

ance and conversion, and not least of all, of concentration on the
essential. With all this seriousness, however, we should not forget
that from the very earliest times, it was also associated with movement in dance and play. Starting from the crane dance of Theseus
and his companions on the isle of Delos, the tradition runs via
the Troy game of the children of Rome to the Easter dance in the
labyrinths of the medieval cathedrals.[12] In Chartres, too, a labyrinth dance was performed by the clergy at Easter vespers to celebrate the victorious resurrection of Christ and the second creation
of the world through him. The labyrinth is thus a representation
of, and guide to, a complex movement from the outside inward
and from the inside back out: a dance figure for body and soul.
The journey toward the interior, the center, was the aspect that
claimed the greater attention during the Middle Ages. This interest

in the mystical journey was revived in another guise in the depth psychology of the twentieth century.[13] Carl Gustav Jung, who has been described as "the lord of the underworld,"[14] used the word "individuation" to describe the mysterious way into the depths. The therapeutic process resembles the dramatic journey that the mystical hero had to go through:

> The labours of the doctor as well as the quest of the patient are directed towards that hidden and as yet unmanifest "whole" man, who is at once the greater and the future man. But the right way to wholeness is made up, unfortunately, of fateful detours and wrong turnings. It is a *longissima via,* not straight but snakelike, a path that unites the opposites . . . whose labyrinthine twists and turns are not lacking in terrors. It is on this *longissima via* that we meet with those experiences which are said to be "inaccessible." Their inaccessibility really consists in the fact that they cost us an enormous amount of effort: they demand the very thing we most fear, namely the "wholeness" which we talk about so glibly and which lends itself to endless theorizing, though in actual life we detour around it in the widest possible circles.[15]

He who ventures courageously into a labyrinth seeking to find the truth of his life is forced by its circuitous pathways to circumambulate the center of himself, to learn to relate with it and to perceive it from all sides. He can only reach it by passing through the entire interior space of the labyrinth beforehand, by relating to all of its dimensions, and integrating them all into the wholeness of his personality. In fact, in a labyrinth all passages lead into each other, making up an interconnected whole. Uninterrupted and leaving no part out, they form the basis for life's adventure of individuation.

Hermann Kern provides the following interpretation in relating such psychic processes to the figure of the labyrinth:

> The labyrinth is thus also a symbol of integration, individuation, of the concentration of all essential layers, aspects, and levels of meaning of a human existence. It

symbolizes, among other things, the process of matura-
tion from a one-dimensional person, fragmented into a
thousand separate functions, into a rounded-out personality, composed in itself, which has found its center.[16]

According to our interpretation, Theseus found in the center
of the Labyrinth the knowledge of the bottomless monstrosity of
human nature. This knowledge caused him to mature and made
him capable, as the Athenians saw it, of ruling the state in a com-
passionate manner. The medieval Christian was meant to follow in
the footsteps of Christ and overtake his Master in the race of life
there in the center of the labyrinth.

Around 1200, at the time the relief representations of labyrinths were fashioned on the church facades at Lucca and Pontremoli, there lived not far away a man who has been referred to as
"the last Christian," Francis of Assisi.[17] I am convinced that in his
person and in the story of his life, we see the symbolism of the
labyrinth take concrete form; but at the same time we see in them
the problematic aspect of medieval Christianity. It is not known if
Francis ever passed through the winding ways of a labyrinth, either
by finger or by foot, but it is sure that, born as the son of a rich
merchant, he carried out the radical change of direction of Christian initiation in real terms and faithfully followed in the footsteps
of Jesus. He lived a life of carefree poverty, not behind monastery
walls but in the midst of the everyday life of the Italian towns, a
life of solidarity with all human beings, of love for the despised
and outcast of urban society, and of brotherly relatedness with all
creatures.

The fascination that emanated from the example of the *poverello* and his companions might have brought about a radical reform of the Church and laid the groundwork for a new culture
based on the spirit of the Gospels if the authorities of the church
and society had let themselves be infected by the effervescent spirit
of the happy pauper: "The free, fraternal, and happy man takes
the place of the man who is fettered to his possessions.[18]

For the feudalized Church, so successfully interested in political power, this was an intolerable provocation, and it was nothing

less for the well-to-do society as a whole, which in the prospering Italian towns was just starting out on the path to capitalism. On the other hand, Francis and his friars minor (lesser brothers) became welcome allies for the papal curia against the threatening poverty movements, against the—in those days—so extraordinarily successful "heretics," when it succeeded in domesticating the revolutionary Franciscan imitators of Jesus into a clericalized order loyal to the Church. Pious and obedient, Francis had no choice but to go along with this.

In the second decade of the thirteenth century, he traveled throughout central Italy as a wandering preacher, and everywhere the church bells rang out to greet him; clerics and believers came out to meet him, shouting with enthusiasm, *Ecco il santo,* "Here comes the saint."[19] After Pentecost in the year 1214, he set out for Spain and succeeded in reaching Santiago de Compostela.

I imagine the following. On his way, Francis also visited the church of San Pietro de Conflentu in Pontremoli, and there this very exemplar of pilgrimhood saw his life symbolized in the image of the labyrinth. His daily practice of a "mystic with open eyes"[20] consisted in finding the presence of his beloved Lord Jesus in a concrete and earthly fashion in the poor and suffering people of the everyday world—not in some sacrosanct solitude, and even less in some contrived absorption in his own inner world.

Francis combined distance from and nearness to the world. In the radicalness of his poverty and celibacy, he remained a stranger to it; in the concrete and real quality of his love he found himself in immediate nearness to the earth and its creatures. In the popular *Fioretti,* he appears as the *servo di Cristo,* as the only legitimate servant of Christ, almost another Christ given to the world for the salvation of the people, who made paradise in the life of this world into a living fact: "the certainty and joy of the blessed are to be enjoyed here on earth."[21] A pity. The rumor of holiness can be deadly for any cause; it can turn it into the business of spokesmen for the holy. What Georges Duby says of the peoples of Aquitania in the twelfth century certainly goes for many of the followers of Saint Francis too: "It was nothing new for them to delegate the vocation of poverty and chastity to others, to depend for it on specialists in salvation, to trust the well-being of their souls to ritual gestures and simultaneously to profit contentedly from the world."[22]

The diagnosis that Carl Gustav Jung made for the twentieth century is not far different:

> The demand made by the *imitatio Christi*—that we should follow the ideal and seek to become like it— ought logically to have the result of developing and ex-alting the inner man. In actual fact, however, the ideal has been turned by superficial and formalistically-minded believers into an external object of worship, and it is precisely this veneration for the object that prevents it from reaching down into the depths of the psyche and giving the latter a wholeness in keeping with the ideal. Accordingly the divine mediator stands outside as an image, while man remains fragmentary and untouched in the deepest part of him. Christ can indeed be imitated even to the point of stigmatization without the imitator coming anywhere near the ideal or its meaning.[23]

In September 1224, on Mount La Verna, Francis experienced stigmatization, the hand wounds resulting from the Crucifixion of his beloved Lord—an ultimate expression of the *imitatio Christi*. Two years later, he had himself laid out naked on the earth, and in honor of his guest and friend, death, had ashes and dust sprinkled over his body, and invited all creatures to join in praising God. Those present heard him saying, in the manner of a host, "Welcome, Brother Death." After sunset, the latter arrived.[24]

Two years after his death, Francis of Assisi was declared a saint and henceforth became a much more comfortable object of veneration and less one of emulation. Anybody in those days who dared, regardless of the official church, to practice a Franciscan spontaneity and spirituality and to draw conclusions from the poverty of Christ ran afoul of the Holy Inquisition, which in 1231 was raised to the dignity of a papal institution. The new mendicant orders eagerly made its mission their own, particularly the Dominicans but also the Franciscans, who had been established as a monastic order. The inflexible among the followers of the *poverello*, the Spirituals, were made to bend by the use of holy violence and then committed to the flames; as *fratizelli*, "little brothers," they vanished from history at the end of the fifteenth century, seemingly forever.[25]

In retrospect, the development of Christianity into its medieval form seems to be the result of a grand-scale misunderstanding. Holy men and women in those days, shut up in the shells of lives regarded as perfect, meditated profoundly on the life of the God become man. They constructed grand theological systems, which were meant to bring human reason closer to the mysteries of God and his creation. Full of devotion, garbed in sumptuous robes, they celebrated the divine liturgy. They inspired the artists—if these did not belong to the spiritual fraternity themselves—to the creation of marvelous edifices, in which the mysteries of the believers were symbolically portrayed. Spirit in abundance. But was it also the Holy Spirit?

Continual new attempts were made to find an answer to the question of the imitation of Jesus. The monks of the Order of Cluny criticized the clergy of the prosperous cathedral chapters, the mendicant monks criticized the rich monasteries of the Benedictine tradition, but one thing remained always the same, even among the supposedly so righteous Dominicans and Franciscans of the thirteenth century, who lived among the public in the cities— ultimately the professionals of the religious life stuck to their own company. It seemed that they had found their way out of the labyrinth of the world into the center; they believed they had found salvation and dwelled within it as on the Isle of the Blessed.

The first known church labyrinth already demonstrated the notion, which though theologically plausible, in practice led time and again into a clerical dead end: the Church, as the mystical body of Christ, is the center of the world, the final goal of all striving. In the Romanesque labyrinth mosaic of the Reparatus Basilica of Orléansville, which was established in 324, we find a serpentine thread of Ariadne running up to the first turn in the way; from there the eye of the observer continues on to the center, where there is a labyrinth of letters, which reads *sancta eclesia,* "holy church."

So there is just this one way: out of the world of pagan error,

Romanesque labyrinth mosaic from the Reparatus Basilica of Orléansville
(El Asnam), today in the cathedral of Algiers.

inward into the truth of the Church—just as in the last medieval
church labyrinth in San Vitale (Ravenna, sixteenth century), there
is only a single pathway leading out of the world of sin. Its direc-
tional arrows point from inside out toward the center of the octagon as the symbolic place of salvation.[26]

What was left for the great mass of Christians who lived in
the world outside the old monasteries and outside the houses of
the new orders without religious privileges other than a graciously
conceded compromise with a world denigrated as sinful? Was there
no valid alternative to this for the imitation of Jesus?

I imagine the following. The pious Christian of Lucca, Pontremoli, or Chartres, who has just meditated on the labyrinth, fails
to find satisfaction in the symbolic ritual. Instead, he adopts pilgrimhood, the state of being continually on the way, as his way of

Concentration

Ravenna, San Vitale: Black-and-white labyrinth of marble under the
dome in one of the eight sectors; laid in the sixteenth century.

life. His brother is Francis, the converted bourgeois, a joyous
stranger in the world of the Establishment, a lover of the divine
creation who lives in solidarity with all its creatures, who laughs
at those who rule and kisses lepers—a dream that was lived for a
short time and which we hope will be renewed as a reality again
and again!

During the years when the last *fratizelli* were being tracked
down by the Inquisition, Christian Europeans swarmed out into a
world as yet unfamiliar to them, yet most of them were not "new
persons" but just the old barbarians. And the monstrous things

that they did in the New World they did with the conviction that they possessed the truth and possessed salvation and that they were obligated to subdue the heathen nations so these too could become like themselves.

SEVEN

The World

The Christian soul in the labyrinth of the world.
Engraving by Boethius von Bolswart (1580–1634),
emblem in Herman Hugo's devotional work *Pia desideria*.

The Labyrinth was a deceptive maze
And so is the world full of trickery and error.
In the middle of the Labyrinth was the gruesome monster,
The child of sin,
The Minotaur;
In the middle of the world is the sworn enemy of God and
*   of humans.*
The thread led unerringly through the maze;
The word of God rightly leads through the world.
Woe be to them
Who deviate from this guideline despite wholesome warning!
The Labyrinth passed away
After Theseus in knightly manner slew that monster
And married the beautiful Ariadne.
Thus despite our reluctance must the world with its pleasure
*   pass away.*
Therefore we supplicate
That this may happen soon,
That God in His strength may release us from evil and all
*   bad things*
And guide us gently and happily into the house of heavenly
*   matrimony*
And crown it with the imperishable crown of stars.

  —ANONYMOUS PROTESTANT, *Nuremberg 1683*

Rinascita, renaissance—the longing of human beings for rebirth and a new beginning continually manifests in religious movements, new directions in culture, and political revolutions. The proclaimed new age is regarded as a return to the good old days, to the origins and wellsprings of communal life, from which human beings—thirsty and frustrated—may draw refreshing drink for the present.

The World

The sense of a new direction prevailed in the Italy of the quattrocento, in the fifteenth century. "Our time" meant for the Italian humanists a new day after the night of the Middle Ages, illuminated by the light of rediscovered ancient art and culture. A new epoch developed that put its program across in repeated fresh expressions: "As the God of this earth, man can do anything he really wants. His deification and sanctification he can best bring about through science, wisdom, magic."[1]

In 1486, Giovanni Pico della Mirandola proclaimed in his tractate *On the Dignity of Man* the self-view of the autonomous subject in the words God says to Adam:

> We created you neither as a heavenly nor an earthly being, neither as a mortal nor an immortal, so that you, as the perfectly free honorary sculptor and poet of yourself, may determine your own form in which you wish to live. You are free to degenerate into the world of beasts. You are equally free to elevate yourself into the higher world of the divine through the resolve of your own mind.[2]

An invention of Leonardo Da Vinci, which he sketched with pen under the heading "mirror," seems like a dramatization of this new self-consciousness. He was not yet technically capable of realizing this invention, but his explanation of it was as follows: "If you make eight flat surfaces, each one two cubits long and three cubits high (1.2 x 1.8 meters), and arrange them in a circle so that they form an octagon with a circumference of sixteen cubits and a diameter of five cubits, then a man inside can see himself infinitely from all sides."

This mirror closet was realized for the first time as the central piece of the Milan labyrinth exhibit of 1981.[3] It seems to me like the leftover center of a labyrinth in whose middle the human being encounters himself in an endless self-reflection. He discovers himself as infinite in his potential and at the same time as a being without any orientation outside of himself. In the infinite reflections of the man inside, the center is surrounded once again by an imaginary labyrinth, which the man, who has become free, experi-

Leonardo da Vinci (1452–1519), *Mirror.* Pen drawing.

ences as a maze. As in the Middle Ages, here again the mystical symbol that is the number eight[4] brings to mind new beginning and perfection, but here it no longer betokens rebirth from water and the spirit, which the Christians in imitation of Jesus placed in the center of the space of salvation, but rather the birth of the self-empowered human being. Leonardo himself embodies this ingenious, titanic human being who is the sculptor and poet of himself, the intellectual *who wants to investigate, comprehend, and make everything.*[5]

It is no accident that it was in the same century that the first labyrinths in the form of mazes were devised,[6] playful innuendoes of the uncertainty of humanity's capacity for orientation and at the same time, signals of a new relationship of man to himself and to the world. In contrast to the medieval labyrinth, which as a figure of orientation and salvation led with certainty into the middle and out again, the new mazes were symbols of a way that was uncertain through and through, on which the traveler constantly had to deal with false paths and confusion, a route that forked without warning and often enough led into dead ends. For the hesitant, they represented an intimidating undermining of certainty; but for the courageous and quick-witted they were an adventurous challenge, a risky game requiring them to locate the goal—the center or the exit—amid the ongoing suspense of trial and error.

Modern labyrinths do not necessarily have a center. Their fixed points are often only entrance and exit—not rarely a number of them—between which the chaos of alternative pathways lies. Where in such a setup could a Minotaur have a place? An intelligent answer to this question was given by Umberto Eco: "A maze requires no Minotaur; it is its own Minotaur. In other words, the attempt of the visitor to find the way is the Minotaur.[7]

In my opinion, the visitor could very well also run into a slightly more abstract Minotaur, namely, being hopelessly confused and feeling one cannot go on—the experience of the dead-end situation. The garden labyrinths of the Renaissance and the Baroque period, the ones made with hedges that were really mazes, served—we should say at once to allay all fears—mainly the playful purpose of easing the need for sociable movement. Finding the solution to them made one forget the boredom of court life, or perhaps every corner of the maze was already known and the maze was a place for a pleasant stroll. But despite the amusement factor, there remained some memory of the medieval play on words *labor intus* ("labor inside") that recalled the toil of earthly existence between birth and death.

Pious Christians were also looking forward to a new time: a change in the world brought about by a thorough reformation of the Church from top to bottom. Martin Luther had called for "a reform of the Christian situation," and Thomas Müntzer, filled with great expectations, for the building of a fraternal Christian communal society. But the spiritual and temporal lords had something else in mind. The mood of religious reform did not take long to expend itself. Reformations and counterreformations, forced conversions and persecutions, wars of faith and witch hunts gave a sinister quality to the illumination of the new time, which was no longer so new. Among Christians, uncertainty and disappointment were widespread.

In such a situation, it is difficult to regard the shape of earthly things as a challenge to faith, love, and hope and, seeing it that way, to accept it. Resignation tempts one to an easier solution, contempt for the world, or failing that, the other extreme— enjoyment of the passing moment, with the motto "after us the deluge." Christian preachers of both persuasions successfully combated the *carpe diem* approach with the long-familiar notion of *contemptus mundi.* The poets, too, hastened to provide assurances:

Ah, what is all this that we hold so precious,
More than worthless nothingness, shadows, dust, and wind,
A wild flower never found again.[8]

The new devaluation of the world found its expression in a characteristic reinterpretation of the maze; or would it be more accurate to say, in a revival of the pessimistic medieval interpretation of the labyrinth?

In that period of great melancholy,[9] at the church of San Savino in Piacenza, an old labyrinth mosaic was still on view, the explanatory text for which has been preserved and in our times has even, through a novel, entered postmodern consciousness:[10]

HUNC MUNDUM TIPICE LABERINTHUS DENOTAT ISTE INTRANTI LARGUS, REDEUNTI SED NIMIS ARTUS SIC MUNDO CAPTUS VICIORUM MOLE GRAVATUS VIX VALET AD VITE DOCTRINAM QUISQUE REDIRE.

This labyrinth is a typical representation of our world— for him who would enter it is wide, but for him who would turn back, quite narrow. Thus he who is caught up in the world, laden with the burden of his sins, is hardly able to return to the teaching of life.

The most outstanding literary formulation of this idea was that of the Czech scholar Jan Amos Koménsky, who is known to educated Europeans by the name Comenius. He wrote his novel *The Labyrinth of the World and the Paradise of the Heart* as a young minister of the Bohemian Brethren, shortly after the beginning of the Thirty Years' War.

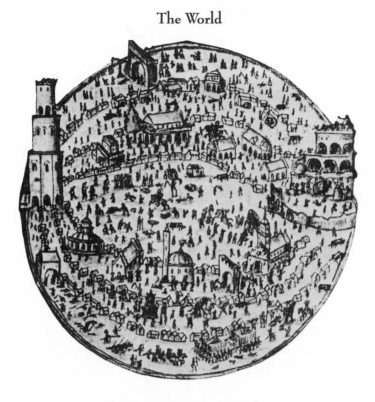

Johan Amos Comenius, *The Labyrinth of the World.*

In 1620, the Catholic faction won the Battle of White Mountain near Prague and set to work imposing its counterreformation by violent means. Koménsky had to abandon his ministry in Fulnek in Moravia and take refuge in Brandeis in East Bohemia. There, in 1622–23, he worked on his *Consolational Writings,* among them *The Labyrinth of the World.* In the spring of 1628, he went into exile in Poland, the refuge of the Bohemian Brethren, and there his work appeared in 1631. A second, enlarged edition was published in Amsterdam, his second place of asylum, in 1663. This was the book of an emigré, a citizen of the world, who said of himself at the end of his life: "My life was a wandering; I never had a homeland. It was a matter of being constantly tossed about, without rest; nowhere and never did I find a home."[11] Comenius commented on the title of his labyrinth book in the following words: "It is a clear description of how in this world and in all the things of this world, nothing prevails besides error and confusion, uncertainty and torment, lying and deception, fear and misery, and ultimately, revulsion toward everything and despair; and how only he who dwells at home in his heart and shuts himself up there alone with God attains the true and full peace of his soul and achieves joy.[12] The author's accompanying hand drawing[13] is a straightforward attempt to show the labyrinth of the world as, to all appearances, a very beautiful, even magnificent and extensive city. A young man wanders through this city in order to gain experience. "Thus I went out from myself, and I began to look around on all sides." Immediately a guide presents himself to him, Omniscient, with the nickname Ubiquitous:

> "Have you heard of the Labyrinth of Crete?"
> "I think so," said I.
> "It was a wonder of the world," he explained, "a building made up of so many chambers, rooms, and passages that whoever ventured into it without a guide, no matter how long he might stray and blunder about therein, would never find an exit. Yet that was only child's play compared to how the labyrinth of the world is formed, especially nowadays. I counsel you, place your trust in an experienced man; don't venture into it alone."

This audacious companion, who is driven by curiosity, is soon joined by another, who is called Delusion. He is the embodiment of prejudice or preconception, which gives the deceptive appearances of the world the illusion of truth. He says of himself, "I am the interpreter for Wisdom, the queen of the world, from whom I have received the office of instructing everyone how the things of the world are to be taken."

To assure his control, he puts a harness on the wanderer and puts a pair of spectacles on him, the lenses of which are cut from the glass of prejudice and framed with the horn rims known as habit. These have the effect of turning all attributes into their opposites; the view they give is that of an upside-down world. But since, fortunately, they sit on the nose a bit crookedly, the pilgrim succeeds every now and then in getting his gaze to pass beneath them, so that he catches a glimpse of things in their natural form.

As a threesome, they wander through the world-city, the showplace of the human drama. Its countless streets, plazas, houses, and neighborhoods are allegories of the various conditions of life. They also reach the Castle of Good Fortune, the Arx Fortunae, where the more eminent people live, enjoying wealth, pleasure, and fame. Everywhere in the reality of his time the pilgrim recognizes the duplicity of the world: behind the beautiful appearances of the city of the theater of the world, he sees lying and hypocrisy, chaos and impermanence, arrogance and conceit, and ultimately, sickness and death. Deeply disappointed, he reproaches his companions in the following terms:

> "You have taken me everywhere, but tell me, how has it helped me? You promised me wealth, peace of mind, and knowledge, but what do I possess of all that? Naught! And what am I capable of? Naught! Where am I? I do not know. I know only one thing, that after so many errant paths and so many toils and so many dangers faced, inwardly I am completely depleted and exhausted and have found nothing other than the pain in my own breast, and with it the hatred of others toward me."

His protest results in his companions taking him to the castle of Wisdom, the queen of the world, and accusing him before the court. However, he is spared and has the bitter pleasure of making the acquaintance of the world's Regiment of Women: the secret councilors of the queen are vices masquerading as virtues such as purity, kindness, probity, bravery; her functionaries are Mrs. Hustlebustle for the lower town and Mrs. Goodfortune for the castle of happiness. To his horror, he also learns that wise King Solomon, who recognized the vanity of the world, has been seduced by sensual pleasures.

When the wanderer, seeking to reach a fundamental understanding of things, finally comes to the end of the world, to where the darkness begins, his companions leave him. Now he flings the spectacles of delusion far from him, rubs his eyes, and sees before him the realm of death, and in it nothing but repulsive worms, toads, snakes, scorpions, and rot; and there is a stench of sulphur and pitch. There body and soul shudder with nameless tortures. The pathways of the labyrinth finally lead to the bottomless abyss beyond the world, so it turns out to be simply a way without an outlet, a dead end in the literal sense. Confronted with the monster of death, with the horrors of outermost darkness, he screams for help: "O God, O God—if there is a God—have mercy on my misery." Then he hears a voice, the voice of God, call out: "Turn back! Go back whence you came, into the little chamber of your heart, and close the door behind you!"

He follows this advice at once. He takes up residence in the chamber of his heart. He finds it dark, chaotic, and confused, but his goodwill is rewarded. Christ appears, and this Visitor becomes for the wanderer returned home everything that the world could not provide: housemate, brother, father, friend, betrothed, the true physician, the higher power that he can serve directly—without being separated from God by the "ceremonies" of the Church.[14] The prerequisite for all of that is only that the wanderer returned home must destroy his self-will, his ego, so that which is the will of God can transpire.

After his rebirth has taken place in this manner, he acquires a new harness, the yoke of obedience, and a new pair of spectacles, the lenses of which are made from the glass of the Holy Ghost, and the frames are the word of God, "a perspective that will enable you, if only you are willing to give it proper heed, to recognize the stupidities of the world, and then also to see the joys of my elect that much more clearly." Equipped in this way, he hastens through the turmoil of the world to the temple of Christ, the place of the *praxis christianismi*. The invisible church is hidden behind a twofold veil: by the dark veil, perceivable from the outside, the *contemptus mundi;* and by the veil perceivable only from the inside, the *amor Christi,* the love of Christ. The *ecclesia spiritualis* is the church of the *inner Christ,* a sacred community where all assemble who have forsworn the world.

Pia desideria, pious longings and wishes, are what were to be aroused in Christians. This is the title of a devotional book by the Jesuit priest Hermann Hugo, which appeared for the first time in 1624 and enjoyed great success.[15] The Christian is in need of wings, that is, longing for the eternal things, in order to rise above the world to holy bliss—so said Comenius. But also very critically expressed wishes were put forth under the title *Pia desideria,* for example, also Philipp Jacob Spener's essay laying out his program for church reform, which became the manifesto of German pietism: *Hertzliches Verlangen Nach Gottgefälliger Besserung der wahren evangelischen Kirchen sampt einigen dahin einfältig abzweckenden Christlichen Vorschlägen* (Heartfelt Longing for a Reformation, Pleasing to God, of the True Evangelical Churches, along with a Few Directly Pertinent Christian Proposals).[16]

What Spener put forward had had the groundwork laid for it almost a half-century earlier by Comenius in his *Paradise of the Heart.* Elsewhere Spener expressed the view that the Reformation had gotten stuck at the halfway point and he accused Protestant scholasticism of obscuring the light of the Gospels.[17] Christian life, for Comenius as for Spener, was a counteraction of the world, a radical alternative. The world—reduced to a metaphor—is a big city in which the market of vanities and the theater of life have their place. Age-old literary themes come together here.[18] The wanderer looks closely at the labyrinth-city; he is not himself an actor in it, just an observer. The experience he has in the course of his tour is nothing other than a progressive disillusionment, which permits him to say no with conviction. But can such a frustrating sightseeing tour, which is turned by the Christian *deus ex machina* into an ascension to heaven, to the "paradise of the heart," be called a journey of initiation?[19]

A glance at spiritual mazes in pictures and written descriptions confirms the view of the world and of life conveyed by literature. A contemporary engraving (see page 85) shows the Christian soul, dressed as a pilgrim standing in the middle of the labyrinth of the world. He is looking up to the castle of heaven, from which an angel is guiding him toward the exit with a ropelike thread of Ariadne, a simile for the word of God. The path runs along the top of high labyrinth walls, from which there is a danger of falling in a moment of unbelief, as has actually happened to two other travelers. By contrast, a blind man with his dog—an image of faith in God—is finding his way with certainty. The beacon fire on the heavenly tower also provides the orientation necessary for ships on the uncertain sea. But even when the ocean and the labyrinth are both overcome, namely, by climbing the mountain of heaven, man is still not safe from falling, as the picture shows. The caption for the engraving is taken from Psalm 119: "O that my ways were directed to keep thy statutes!" In the commentary accompanying the emblem in the German version of the *Pia desideria* of 1719, we read:

> In the confused maze
> All made of crooked ways
> I walk, and will wait without fear
> For the help Your Word promises.
> From far I see that here and there some fall
> Who otherwise are careful enough, even the most capable.
> I walk on blindly and my whole art consists
> In abandoning myself entirely to you, my Friend! . . .
>
> He who would base himself upon his own strength
> On his skill, on his nimbleness,
> Will find in his pride
> That he has gone far wide of the way. . . .
> This life is a maze.
> For your way in it to be sure
> You must without falsity wait upon God with blind faith
> With pure love, without hypocrisy.[20]

EIGHT

The Journey of Life

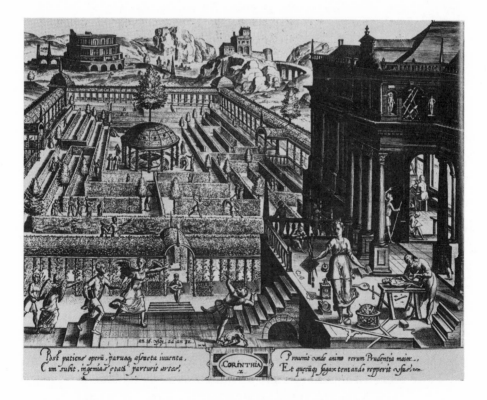

Hedge Maze. Engraving by Hieronymus Wierix, Antwerp, c. 1600.

Man's journey through life is like a path that strays.
A child goes astray out of simplicity, a wise man through
  desire,
Age's false path is falsely propped delusion,
The glittering ore of miserliness, the strange ornament
  of lust.
Every vice misses and deviates from the middle,
Seeks a side path to ruination.
Yea, not one in a hundred knows his way to the grave.
The need to die he knows but not the way.

Yet he who strays through this edifice with reason
Will find his path to salvation, the guiding thread
  of truth. . . .

> —Daniel Casper von Lohenstein,
> "Inscription for a Labyrinth"

At the same time as the pious of the land—with their very medieval frame of mind—were formulating their renunciation of the world, others were being inspired by the worldly cast of humanistic thought. My understanding of the hedge maze depicted by Hieronymus Wierix (page 97)[1] is as follows. Among the visitors to the garden—musicians, strolling couples, and individuals—the most noticeable are the dueling youths in the foreground, people in the "labyrinthine," immature stage of life between sixteen and thirty-two, as the commentary on the picture says. Angels lead them to the palace of the fine arts, where they are received by Prudentia, (insight and cleverness). In the background of the picture, we recognize the ruins of the Tower of Babel, a reminder of the Babylonian confusion of languages, thus an allusion to the new age's uncertainty of mind—the reverse side of its new freedom, as expressed in the model of the maze. A contemporary, Baltasar Gracián, in his satirical novel, *El Criticón,* calls it a Babel of disorder.[2]

The Journey of Life

Does it have to be angels who guide human beings out of the dead ends of human existence? In his didactic poem "Aufschrift eines Labyrinths" (Inscription for a Labyrinth), Daniel Casper von Lohenstein takes the point of view that human life resembles a path going astray, but he shows his Christian contemporaries a new perspective, which was not to find acceptance before the eighteenth century:

> Yet he who strays through this edifice with reason
> Will find his path to salvation,
> The guiding thread of truth.[3]

The new century, in which reason was to be declared the guiding thread of human thought and action, was called by Immanuel Kant the "age of enlightenment." By this he meant the point in history at which "the departure of humanity from its self-imposed minority" began.[4] The basic model for this is: "the obligation and right of parents to control and educate the child for as long as it is not capable of independent use of its own limbs and likewise of its understanding" come to an end with its release *(emancipatio)* into majority.[5] Can such a sudden leap into the freedom of self-determination actually be realized?[6] The paradoxical advice to "stray with reason" seems to have its point of application precisely here. The moment that the Baroque and Rococo garden labyrinth constructed in a geometrical style—the intellectual pleasure garden— was superseded by the just as artificially arranged naturalness of the English garden, literature definitively adopted the depiction and interpretation of the labyrinth as an expression of "Life's perplexing Labyrinth."[7] What modern humanity was thought to have in store for it is demonstrated in exemplary fashion by Homunculus, the little man in the test tube, in the Classical Walpurgis Night in Goethe's *Faust:*

> HOMUNCULUS
> From point to point I float around
> Longing impatiently to break my glass
> And join the fullness of creation;
> Only the things I have seen so far, alas,
> I would not join without some trepidation.
> . . . .

MEPHISTOPHELES
Unless you err, naught can be truly known.
If life you want, then find it as your own.

HOMUNCULUS
Such good advice is not a thing to flout.[8]

Homunculus finally follows the advice of old Thales to begin his evolution all the way from the beginning, with the element of water. The pessimistic commentary of Proteus:

> For at the state of man arriving
> Finished and damned is your career

is countered by Thales with the remark:

> That all depends: it can be much
> To be a man of mettle, famed as such.[9]

That which Homunculus will have to wait a few million years for comes unexpectedly fast and seemingly perfectly to Goethe's Wilhelm Meister,[10] after just a few turbulent years of apprenticeship. By no means did young Wilhelm have in mind, after his "release into majority," to travel roundabout and errant paths. Rather, he thought he had already reached his goal in having found the actress Mariane, his first love, as the woman of his life, and in thinking that with her he could realize his childhood dream of a career in the theater. But in what follows, everything goes wrong, or at least so it seems. Not only, in order to continue on his way, does he have to escape the labyrinth of his feelings, which continue to try to seduce him, but his outer circumstances also take on a quality of labyrinthine confusion. In his self-development, he is only helped in a limited way by the "Tower Society," a secret group of the type of the Freemasons, whose members, tried and seasoned by life, practice a modern variant of Ariadne's thread. And then the country pastor, a spokesman for an unabashedly worldly spirituality, provides us with the following food for thought: "To keep a person from error is not the duty of the educator, but rather to lead on him who errs, indeed, to make him slurp his error from a full cup; that is the wisdom of the teacher."

Error, so it would seem, can only be cured by erring. Nothing is in vain; for everything we encounter leaves traces; everything contributes imperceptibly to our development. Thus Wilhelm Meister comes closer and closer to the fulfillment of the wish he has harbored unwittingly from the time of his childhood and to his ever more consciously desired goal: "to develop myself just as I am." At the end of the novel, when the burgher's son received his apprenticeship certificate and finds in the noble Natalie the real woman of his life, he hears his years of apprenticeship summarized: "You seem to me like Saul, the son of Kish, who went out looking for his father's asses and found a kingdom."

Goethe's novel depicts a modern version of the initiation process. Wilhelm Meister treads the convoluted path of initiation into life by relating to the people and events—for the most part unsought and unexpected, but of the profoundest relevance for him—that he encounters. For after all, as an insightful interpreter of it said, life is "not the expected, the planned, but rather that which turns up, the other, the alien; yet ultimately this is one's own, corresponding in an inexplicable and obscure manner to the self, whether in the end it fosters this self or destroys it."[11]

Another point of view was that of Novalis, one of the geniuses of Romanticism, whose teacher was Goethe, yet who felt an ineluctable need to distance himself from him:

> Against *Wilhelm Meisters Lehrjahre*. It is basically a fatalistic and silly book. . . . At last everything becomes a farce. Economic nature is the true remaining thing. . . . The whole thing is a nobility novel. *Wilhelm Meisters Lehrjahre,* or The Pilgrim's Journey to the Nobility Diploma.[12]

The Romantic's antithesis is found in the novel *Henry of Ofterdingen,* which appeared unfinished in 1802, after the author's premature death and six years after Goethe's *Wilhelm Meister.* For Henry, the medievally costumed protagonist of the novel, life is a pilgrimage to a holy grave, to which dreams, as divine provender for the journey, kindly accompany him.[13] In Novalis's book of fragments, *Pollen,* we learn how this pilgrimage takes place:

We dream of voyages through the universe. But isn't the universe *in us?* We do not know the depths of our minds—the mysterious way runs inward. In us or no-where is eternity with its worlds—the past and the fu-ture.[14]

It is not surprising that the novel begins immediately with a dream. This leads young Henry into a cave, where an epiphany—a dream within a dream—symbolically reveals to him the goal of life's journey:

A kind of sweet slumber came over him, in which he dreamed of indescribable things, and from which he was awakened by another epiphany. He found himself on a soft lawn at the end of a spring, which gushed into the air and seemed to consume itself there. Dark blue cliffs with colorful veins rose at some distance. The daylight around him was clearer and softer than usual daylight; the sky was very dark blue and completely pure. But what drew him with complete power was a light blue flower, which stood close to the spring and touched him with its broad, shining petals. Around it grew countless flowers of all colors, and the most delicious odor filled the air. He saw nothing but the blue flower and looked at it for a long time with a nameless tenderness.[15]

Henry is just twenty years old when he sets out on his jour-ney. His way soon takes him to the mining folk who live at the foot of a mountain range. An old miner—people call him a treasure digger—tells him of the art of mining, describing it as a symbol of human life. It opens the way to the hidden treasure chambers of nature through a maze of passages. The miner's fellows seem to him, as he reveals,

like subterranean heroes who have to overcome a thou-sand perils but also possess the enviable good fortune of wondrous knowledge, and in solemn, still companion-ship with the age-old rock sons of nature in their won-drous chambers, are made ready to receive heavenly gifts and be lifted joyously above the world and its tor-ments.

He assures the enthusiastically listening Henry that his work in the interior of the earth has brought him into full possession of what has always been his fondest wish:

> This full satisfaction of an inborn wish, this miraculous joy in things, which may have a close relationship to our secret existence, to occupations for which we have been destined and prepared from the cradle, cannot be described and explained.

As if there were a need to prove what he has said in practice, one evening the old man guides the society of merchants, which Henry has joined, into nearby caves, into the interior of the earth. In the deepest vault, they are amazed to discover a hermit, who in conversation shows himself to be equally well-versed in matters of the outer world as of the inner life. Through this meeting, Henry feels himself transformed in his inmost being: "Many a word, many an idea, fell on him like life-giving pollen and transported him swiftly out of the narrow confines of his youth onto the peak of the world." Left alone for a while by the others, among the books the hermit shows him, he finds a truly wonderful one, which draws his full attention. It is written in a language that Henry does not understand, and there is no title to give a hint of its contents. Only a few pictures speak to him:

> They struck him as familiar in a quite wondrous fashion, and when he looked closely, he discovered his own figure, quite recognizable among the others. He became frightened and thought he was dreaming, but after repeated examination, he was no longer able to doubt the perfect likeness. He hardly trusted his senses when, soon, he came across a picture of the cave and the hermit and the old man next to himself. . . . A great number of the figures he was unable to name, yet they struck him as familiar. He saw this likeness of him in various situations. Toward the end, he seemed to himself to be larger and more noble. . . . The end of the book seemed to be missing.

Henry is unable to read the enigmatic book, but the pictures speak to him, and he looks at them again and again, until he hears the society of merchants coming back. From the hermit, he learns that the book is written in the Provençal language, and that it is a novel of the wonderful adventures of a poet in which the art of writing is depicted and praised in its many aspects. And the mysterious hermit adds, "The conclusion of this manuscript, which I brought back from Jerusalem, is missing."

Memory and premonition come together in a mysterious interplay. In the depths of the cave, he leafs through his life in the book and sees in pictures and signs the future as if it were the past. Is the end still open, undecided? Will Henry, who feels the vocation of a writer, reach the goal of his dream "for which he was destined and prepared from the cradle"? The book of his life, written in Jerusalem, must, according to its own logic, also come to an end there. Is it the heavenly Jerusalem, which the pious Christians of all times have longed for, or the one that the person of the new age seeks in the depths of the soul? The naive, instinctive sureness with which Henry approaches his seemingly earth-transcending goal is more a wish than a certainty:

> . . . should not that childlike and guileless simplicity be surer in hitting on the way through the labyrinth of present-day realities than cleverness, which is inhibited and led astray by concern for advantage and bedazzled by an inexhaustible number of new coincidences and complications?

For Novalis, an example of this kind of clever traveler clearly is Wilhelm Meister on his pilgrimage to a nobility diploma. His development seems to move through a horizontally conceived maze. The goal of his education seems to be lacking any dimension of depth; it is a superficial compromise with the reality of his day. So, is Goethe's novel a description of an initiation that leads only to the banality of social and "economic" reality?[16]

The alternative way is the one Henry is destined for. He is "hardly more than a leap from the way of inner contemplation." The realities he encounters on his journey, the stories and fairy tales that are told him—everything that comes to him from the outside is only a spur for the inner process of development he experiences. "Everything he saw and heard seemed only to push aside the bolts of locks within him and to open new windows before him." And in another place, we read, "The heartening spectacle of the magnificent evening nurtured gentle fantasies within him: at moments the flower of his heart made itself visible within him like a glimmer of lightning." There do not seem to be any false, misleading paths here—only the goal-sure, yet roundabout way to the center, the path into the depths, leading into the mine shafts of the interior,[17] into the paradise of the heart. "Where then are we going? Always home." Initiation is for the Romantic "hardly more than a leap" into the space of infinity, into the dimension of the absolute, into purely poetic being. In contrast, Wilhelm Meister must declare: "A human being does not become happy until his unconditional striving itself sets a limit to itself."[18]

Humanity's yearning remains to find the blue flower. Novalis's novel remained a fragment; his life was ended by an early death.

Joseph von Eichendorff's "Song of the Life Journey of Two Companions" sounds like a final lament for the different views of life portrayed in the two, Classical and Romantic, novels:

> Two lively companions set out
> From home for the first time,
> Sallied joyously into the brilliant
> Ringing, singing waves
> Of full-ripe spring.
>
> They sought after high things.
> Whatever the pleasure and pain, they wanted
> To make something right happen in the world,
> And whomever they passed,
> Senses and heart laughed within him.
>
> The first one found a darling,
> In-laws bought them house and land.
> Soon he was rocking a baby boy
> And gazing from cozy hearthside
> Comfortably out over the field.
>
> To the second sang deceivingly
> The thousand voices of the ground,

Alluring sirens, and drew him
Into the amorous waves
Of the colorfully ringing abyss.

And when he surfaced from the abyss
He was old and tired.
His little ship had run aground,
Dead quiet was all around,
And over the water a cold wind blew.

The waves of springtime
Sing and ring over me.
Seeing such bold companions
Fills my eyes with tears—
O God, in your love, guide us to You.[19]

Youth sallying forth with longing ends in the dead end of grown-up life. In the case of the first lad—a Biedermeier-like parody of Wilhelm Meister—youth lands unexpectedly in the prosaic existence of a possessor of wife and child, house and land. Lofty ideals end not in reasonable self-limitation, but in the narrow confines of the bourgeois pursuit of happiness. The second youth—who only remotely recalls the dreamer Henry of Ofterdingen—follows the siren song of his own depths and loses himself in the abyss of the infinite, in the ruinous intoxication of self-illimitation. It seems that the right kind of life cannot be found anywhere. Lay the blame at God's feet! Is this gentle request for divine guidance an expression of resignation on the part of the late Romantic, or a sign of the wisdom of a Christian poet?

Just a hundred years later, even the mildest request for support has been extinguished, and the wandering pathways of life have turned into a single dead end:

"Ah," said the mouse, "the world grows narrower with every passing day. At first it was so wide that I was afraid. I ran on and was happy finally to see walls on the left and right in the distance, but these long walls rushed toward each other so fast, that I am already in the last room, and there in the corner is trap that I am about to run into."

"You have only to change direction," said the cat, and ate it.[20]

NINE

The Garden of Love

Guide to the Way to Marriage out of the Labyrinth of Flirtation.
Engraving used as an illustration to a poem of the
Dutch poet Jacob Cats (1577–1660).

Yes these the eyes, yes these the lips,
That gazed in mine, that gave the kiss,
The fair round body, slender hips,
As formed for Paradise's bliss.
Was she here? Where did she go?
Yes! she it was, she who gave,
Gave herself as away she flew,
And made all my life her slave.

—JOHANN WOLFGANG VON GOETHE,
West-Eastern Divan

"Flee also youthful lusts!" the apostle Paul once warned Timothy.[1] Just about six hundred years later, a Dutch engraver made this very Paulinian imperative into the motto of his labyrinth of love, intended as an illustration for a poem of his compatriot Jacob Cats. The engraving was called "Guide to the Way to Marriage out of the Labyrinth of Flirtation."[2] The strict Protestants of the day surely took this motto as a spur to open their bibles to the rest of what the rigorous apostle had to say:

> From such turn away. For of this sort are they which creep into houses, and lead captive silly women laden with sins, led away with diverse lusts. Ever learning, and never able to come to the knowledge of the truth.[3]

In fact, do women ever come to a knowledge of the truth at all? one is tempted to ask. A glance at the image in the engraving gives us the answer of the seventeenth century. A fashionably dressed young woman with a bouquet of flowers in her hand enters a maze of hip-high hedges, led on by Amor. In the passages stroll various couples. Only one man has remained without a woman companion. In the middle of the labyrinth, in a trellis-work pergola set up around a maypole sits a convivial group: a wedding is being celebrated. Near the entrance, Amor, who is leading the young woman by a thread of Ariadne, shows the way with promising gestures into the labyrinth, toward where, at the next turning, the single man is waiting, ready for a rendezvous.

The sense of this setup is clear enough for the observer; any commentary is really superfluous. Nevertheless, a commentary is given in the four medallions. Above left we have a couple by a signpost, in front of a labyrinth; below left there are two calves; and above right, Amor on a calf, an allusion to calves' love, the flirtation. Below right is the very hand of God, with Ariadne's thread, showing the way through a forest.[4]

"Flee also youthful lusts!" No one is spared passage through the labyrinth of flirtation, or young love, who wishes to reach the goal. One twists and turns, runs into obstacles, gets confused. If everything goes well, marriage brings the knowledge of the truth. It is the cure for youthful lusts and the paradisiacal place or fertility, where the tree of life grows.

A contemporary, Michel de Montaigne, gives a striking description of the sought-after state:

> The state of marriage is a pious, sacred bond. That is the reason why the pleasure that is drawn from it must be a pleasure that is measured, solemn, and mixed with a degree of strictness. It must to some extent be an intelligent and conscientious sensuality. And because its principal purpose is preservation and procreation, there are some who cast doubt on the permissibility of desiring this proof of love when the accomplishment of this ultimate goal cannot be hoped for.[5]

In 1600 in civilized Europe, love labyrinths were very popular. What was their fascination? Clearly, not so much the idea of the end result, a proper marriage, but more the enjoyment of the way to it. The pretext of moral rectitude made possible the development of playful alternatives. Instead of steering resolutely for the harbor of matrimony, one sailed for Cythera, the island of Aphrodite; before one ended up in the Garden of Eden, the Paradise of Love, the hedge labyrinth offered all sorts of occasions for hiding away and engaging in preliminary delectations. If conscience caught the joyriding imagination in the midst of forbidden adventures, the labyrinth of love had a correspondence for that experience as well. Instead of having tasted of the fruit of the tree of life, one found oneself beneath the tree of the knowledge of good and evil with the fatal apple in one's hand, and most surely, it had been picked by some Eve. Being cast out of paradise and having to face the toils of life were the bitter result.

The "Trojan Castles"[6] of the north were an entirely different sort of garden of love—if indeed they were not simply representations of prosaic magical fish traps, used by Scandinavian fishermen to bring about a successful catch. Reports of the erotic nature of the Trojan Castles are somewhat doubtful, but this fact should not prevent us from looking into them. "Trojan Castle" was the name for labyrinth-shaped stone structures, made of stones ranging in size from that of a fist to that of a head, which are laid out unmortared in an open field. In their construction, they are Cretan, that is to say, pre-Christian labyrinths. They have fantastic names: Round Castle, Giant's Fence, Giant's Road, Stonewall, and also city names, like Jerusalem, Nineveh, Babylon, Jericho, Constantinople, and Lisbon. A few of them are called *Jungfrudans,* Maidens' Dance, and Stone Dance. In spite of their expressive names, they are mute witnesses of the past. Their origin is thought to go back a thousand years or more. The earliest indication of their significance comes from a fresco of the fifteenth century in the church of Sibbo in Nyland, Finland. It shows a woman in the middle of a labyrinth.[7]

The most recent evidence comes from an eighty-year-old Finnish woman, who in 1985 recounted her experiences as a child at a Trojan Castle:

> In the center of it stood a girl, whom a young man was to try to reach. In doing this, he dared not make a false step, and could not step on the stones or lose his balance in moving through the maze. . . . During the game, the spectators stood around the edge of the labyrinth, clapping their hands and singing. When the young man reached the center, he had to pick the girl up and carry

Church of Sibbo. Woman in the Labyrinth.

her out of the labyrinth. If he succeeded, the girl be-longed to him.[8]

An old man had another name for such a labyrinth: maiden's ring, he called it. According to his recollection, a girl stood in the center, but in this case it was two different young men who came from different entrances and competed to reach the middle, both trying to be the first to reach the pretty young woman and win her.[9]

The motif of the woman in the labyrinth appears in two different versions. In one case, a woman is carried off and held prisoner in the labyrinth until she is freed, as happened to beautiful Helen in the Trojan War. In the other case, a girl is liberated by a young man who manages to get through to where she is, a version we are familiar with from "Sleeping Beauty."

The woman in the labyrinth: should we not also think of the biblical story of the harlot Rahab, whose life was spared at the taking of Jericho, because she hid the two Israelite scouts and let them down from the top of the city wall on a rope. Jericho was, for the medieval book illustrators, the city with a sevenfold ring of

Jericho as a luniform labyrinth. Colored miniature on parchment in a
composite manuscript of the twelfth century from Saint Emmeran,
Regensburg, Germany.

walls, a true labyrinth—though in the Book of Joshua, the only
allusion to this is that the Israelites went around the city seven
times before they blew their horns for the attack.[10] Rahab received
from the two spies a scarlet thread, which she tied to her window.
It was to be the thread that would lead to the rescue of herself and
her family, an expression of gratitude for the rope with which she
had saved the foreigners.[11]

A scarlet thread. Could the thread of Ariadne also have been
of this color? It had to be highly visible, otherwise Theseus would

have been unable to find his way with its help. But perhaps that is
completely the wrong explanation. A number of the Greek accounts take the view that Theseus had to light the darkness of the
Labyrinth in order to reach his goal. For this reason, the thread of
Ariadne does not appear in these stories; instead the way is lit by a
radiant diadem. But it was Ariadne who possessed such a diadem.
Was it the bridal garland that she received from her legitimate husband Dionysus, or the garland with roses woven into it that was
Amphitrite's gift, and which Theseus may have given to the amorous woman as a gesture of greeting? In any case, the story tells
us that Ariadne accompanied the hero in his passage through the
Labyrinth.

What may have happened there in the dim sidereal glow of
the divinely given garland is a mystery, like everything else that has
come down to us about the Labyrinth. Certainly the Bull of Minos
must have died, but then, immediately thereafter, a marriage was
celebrated—a sacred marriage, a *hierosgamos,* to be sure—a celebration of fertility, of the beginning of new life. In this marriage,
the lover from Athens played the role of Dionysus, the true mate
of Ariadne. But for Theseus, this was the appearance of Aphrodite,
the goddess of love, Ariadne Aphrodite.[12]

A truly sacred cohabitation, then! The notion of violation of
wedlock simply must be ruled out here, even though after the event
there may have been a great deal of talk about it. Much more to
the point here is the notion of representation. Theseus represents
Dionysus; and not only him, but also Minos, the Cretan *paredros*
of the goddess, whether she is now called Pasiphae or Ariadne Aphrodite; and Theseus does this as an official duty—not out of private
pleasure, but as the princely envoy from Athens to Crete.[13]

Later commentaries to the effect that Theseus was the Don
Juan of antiquity, are therefore off the mark. The *hierosgamos,* the
sacred marriage, was above all *sacred,* and therefore only pleasur-
able in a very limited way, as an authoritative scholar of Greek
religion reliably assures us. As the story of Jason, who was killed
by lightning in parallel circumstances, proves adequately, this was
"closer to a sacrifice . . . than a pleasure."[14] Seen in this way, the
sacral cohabitation of Theseus and Ariadne anticipates Christian

Theseus fights the Minotaur accompanied by Ariadne.
Gold relief, c. 650 BC.

Oinochoe (wine pitcher) from Tragliatella (detail). Etruscan, c. 620 BC.
Oldest known representation of the Troy game. The labyrinth, out of which
the two riders are coming, runs to the left and is labeled "Truia."

marriage as it was described by Michel de Montaigne in the six-teenth century, "a pious, sacred bond (which allows only) a plea-sure that is measured, solemn, and mixed with a degree of strictness."[15]

The later European tradition tended to follow the profane interpretation of the events in the Labyrinth, which the more suc-cessful tales of the Greeks transmitted to us. First of all, Theseus had to prove himself—kill the Bull of Minos, and find his way out of the Labyrinth. Only then does Ariadne become serious, and she lets herself be taken by storm. Fertility is a lesser requisite here. A distant reminder of the bullfighters and the twofold victor Theseus are the ancient *ludi taurini*, bull games, which used to take place on the first of May in the mountains of León. Young men who wore bull horns on their heads fought with each other for the young women. At the end, the latter went off to the haystacks with the winners. The couples stayed together for half a year, then separated.[16] Unfortunately, such a period of love was not granted to our classical couple.

As a contrast to the earthy folk customs of the old days in Europe, we have the mind games of the poets and thinkers. It is not without deeper reasons that since the time of the Renaissance the great days of the Labyrinth have been closely bound up with a great interest in eroticism and sexuality. Even such an idea as *pansexuality* has been bruited about.[17] The tradition runs from Gianbattista Marino—who is said, with his epic *L'Adone,* to have set the sexual avalanche in motion—down to the novels of Henry Miller in the twentieth century. Leonardo da Vinci had already referred to love as *terribile e suave,* "terrible and sweet," a paradoxical, and at the same time, labyrinthine experience. Marino went a step further in speaking of it as a "modern monster" in which all opposites were united:

> Deliberate madness, pleasurable evil,
> Tired peace, corrupt benefice.
> Desperate hope, living death,
> Bold fear, tormented laughter,
> Indestructible glass, incandescent ice:
> Eternal abyss of discordant concord,
> Hellish paradise, heavenly hell.[18]

Discord and concord in one make a real mongrel like the Minotaur, the animal-man with divine ambitions. Yet it is not only a monstrous condition, but also, and above all, a labyrinthine state of affairs, a modern maze.

The cryptic paradoxical essence of love does not keep Amor's worshipers from mostly praising its sweet side:

The Garden of Love

> But pleasure remaineth the sugar of this time,
> What, more than it, could sweeten life's journey?

So wrote the poet Christian Hofmann von Hoffmannswaldau in the wake of Marino.[19] And yet the following skeptical words were deemed suitable for the Inscription for a Labyrinth: "Man's journey through life is like a path that strays."[20] The love labyrinth of that time expressed visually the experience conveyed by literature, though for the most part with all the Paulinian reservations of Christian morality.

More than a hundred years later, on the threshold of the nineteenth century, Friedrich Schlegel, an intellectual of the Romantic generation, provoked his seemingly enlightened contemporaries in his novel *Lucinde* by having the labyrinthine "apprenticeship years of manhood" lead to the ideal modern marriage. In 1799 it was the scandal of the year in Berlin. Right in the first chapter, Julius writes to Lucinde:

> All the mysteries of the feminine and the masculine spirit seemed to hover around me, as in my solitude suddenly your true presence and the glow of burgeoning joy on your face set me completely aflame. Wit and charm now began their interplay and became the common pulse of our united life force; we embraced each other with the same uninhibited joy with which we would embrace religion.[21]

In his subsequent *Dithyrambischen Fantasie über die schönste Situation* (Dithyrambic Fantasy about the Most Wonderful Situation), contemporaries, if they had not already closed the book with revulsion after the first pages, read the following outrageous sentences:

> Yes! I would have held it for a fairy tale that such joy and such love exist as I now feel, and such a woman, who is at the same time the tenderest lover and the best company and also a perfect friend. . . . It is all part of you, and we are for each other the closest, each the one who understands the other the best. You accompany me through all the stages of human existence, from the most

uninhibited sensuality to the most spiritual intellectuality. Thus the religion of love binds our love ever more intimately and closely together.[22]

Here the paradoxes of the "modern monster" of which Marino had spoken seem to be entirely forgotten. The opposites have fused into a complete synthesis: "They were totally given over to each other and united, and yet each was completely himself, more than he had ever before been, and each utterance was replete with the deepest feeling and the most personal essence."[23]

In the course of a century, the Romantic love marriage became the religion of enlightened society and the model for marriage altogether. Was it really to succeed?[24] Skeptical, the young Heinrich Heine wrote:

> How deep we were wrapped in each other's life,
> Yet how well we behaved, flawlessly moral;
> How often we played at man and wife,
> With never a blow or the sign of a quarrel.
> We sported together in joy and in jest
> And tenderly kissed and so sweetly caressed;
> And finally playing like children that go
> At hide and seek in the woodland together,
> We managed to stray and to hide ourselves so
> That each of us now is lost to the other.[25]

Did they overlook the hand of God, who with the thread of Ariadne shows the way through the woods? Or is it that in the forest labyrinth of the Romantic period, the helpful pointing finger is sought in vain? The elder Goethe gave the experience of the labyrinth of love another cast:

> The most wondrous book of all books
> Is the Book of Love;
> Attentively I have read it:
> Of joys, a few pages,
> Whole sheaves of sorrows;
> One whole part is separation,
> Reunion a slim chapter,
> Fragmentary. Volumes of cares,

The Garden of Love

With clarifications appended,
Endless beyond measure.
O Nisami!—yet in the end,
You found the right way.
The insoluble—who solves it?
Lovers reuniting.[26]

TEN

The Library

Knot with seven nodes. Woodcut by Albrecht Dürer (1471–1528)
following prototypes by Leonardo da Vinci, 1506–1507.

"The Library is a labyrinth!"
"Hunc mundum tipice labyrinthus denotat ille,"
the old man recited, absently. "Intranti largus, redeun-
ti sed nimis artus. The library is a great labyrinth, sign
of the labyrinth of the world. You enter and you do
not know whether you will come out. You must not
transgress the Pillars of Hercules. . . ."
—UMBERTO ECO, *The Name of the Rose*

In the history of the labyrinth there are high points and low points, times of heightened interest and times of oblivion, as in all things human. Often enough it has not been the deep meaning of the phenomenon but its entertaining surface that has preserved it in people's minds to be awakened again and again to new signifi-cance—our childlike pleasure in exciting stories and interesting games. Labyrinthine pathways, whatever form they take on, are always a lure to dancelike movement—what childlike mentality could resist it—and in this there is no dependence on symbolism whatever. Thus Karl Kerényi has spoken of the pagan and worldly "pleasure in the labyrinth," the very thing that continued to live on as an unconscious background tradition in Christian England.[1] However, by 1922 even in that form it seemed to be dying out. In any case, at that time, William Henry Matthews, author of the book *Mazes and Labyrinths,* voiced the opinion that the time of the labyrinths was over and would not revive again.[2] Although much spoke for this view, he turned out to be wrong. For in the 1970s a renaissance of labyrinths and mazes began, which reached a high point in England in 1984 and remains lively today. This renaissance even produced a periodical exclusively concerned with labyrinths. It was called *Caerdroia: The Journal of Mazes and Lab-yrinths,* named for the Welsh for the labyrinth name "City of Troy." The year 1991 was even named International Year of the Labyrinth.[3]

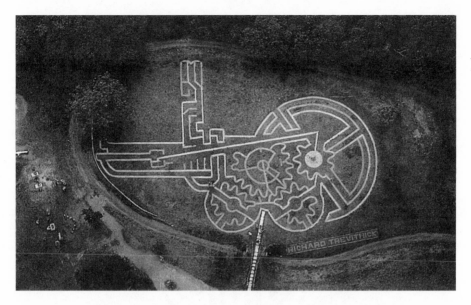

Lappa Maze in Cornwall, a representation of the first locomotive,
constructed by Richard Threvithick in the year 1804.
Used by permission of Georg Gerster, Zumikon-Zürich.

From 1975, a significant role in this movement was played by the firm Minotaur Designs, founded by the British maze designers Randoll Coate and Adrian Fisher, who became well known for their imposing new creations in the genre, like the Lappa Maze, in the form of the world's first railroad steam locomotive, and the enigmatic "Dragon Labyrinth" in Newquay Zoo in Cornwall.[4]

Was it the need for play on the part of the ennui-ridden people of the affluent societies of the second half of the twentieth century that produced this boom, or is there more to it than that? Adrian Fisher, who tried to solve this riddle, expressed the opinion that the visual stimulation and the physical experience of walking within the maze alone do not explain the mystery of the extraordinary fascination of the labyrinth phenomenon.[5] For the mass society man and woman, it is already a beneficial thing to be moving on foot in a protected area that cars cannot get into, to enter such an oasis of quiet and pass a leisure moment in undisturbed convivi-

Hedge maze in Värmlands Säby (Sweden) by Randoll Coate:
the labyrinth in the form of a falcon's egg, symbolized the Garden
of Eden. Adam, Eve, and the Sun are shown in light gray,
the tree of life and the snake in black.

ality. Beyond that, do they experience the hidden meaning of the
labyrinth's structure? The maze designers of our day often base
their creations directly on a specific symbolism. Randoll Coate,
for example, in 1979 in his complex hedge maze "Creation" in
Värmland, Sweden, combined the maze idea with other motifs: the
cosmic egg, paradise, the tree of life, Adam and Eve.[6]

The visitor would have to be able to get a bird's-eye view of
the layout to get even a hint of these symbolic forms. But just walking through the convoluted pathways, he or she perhaps feels a
sense of the basic idea of the maze: that at the root of the confusion

there is an order, which enables the wayfarer to find the thread of Ariadne that leads to the goal. This symbolizes the hope of orientation in a world of which it has become impossible to achieve an overview.

At the beginning of modern times, not only were the first mazes devised but also other forms, which were similar to them in intention, were produced: complex knots that gave the impression of an irresolvable tangle but in reality depicted a single continuous line; however, this line runs in such a way that it feeds without beginning and end back into itself. Leonardo da Vinci and Albrecht Dürer drew this sort of interwoven pattern (see page 119).[7] They were called "maps of mystery" and were cryptographic symbols of the age-old cosmological conception of the cosmic knot, which were drawn with the idea of restoring the unity of a dissolving world through an abstract form.[8] Are we in a situation similar to Leonardo's today?

What is expressed in the successful works of the maze designers might have a parallel in the literature of the 1980s—especially in the world bestseller, the medieval novel *The Name of the Rose*,[9] written by Umberto Eco, who really deserves the title "literature designer." The fictive introduction of the editor is headed "Naturally, a manuscript," and is dated 5 January 1980. The epigraph of the whole novel, taking a corresponding form, could read, "Naturally, a labyrinth"!

William of Baskerville, interpreter of signs and seeker of traces, is confronted immediately on his arrival at the medieval Benedictine abbey on the south slope of the Appenines with an ominous death. It seems that a young monk has been killed by a fall from the east tower of the monastery's Aedificium. He either fell or was pushed from a window of the top story, where the library is located. In a conversation with the abbot, William, who is a Franciscan and a former inquisitor, is asked to clarify the case but learns that in his detective work he must face an uncrossable boundary. Access to the library, which is "spoken of with admiration in all the abbeys of Christendom,"[10] is strictly forbidden not only to visitors of the abbey, but even to its monks, with the exception of the librarian and his assistant. A bizarre taboo!

The Library

"Our library is not like the others,"[11] the abbot explains, and William thinks he is speaking to the meaning of this remark when he praises its incomparable greatness:

> I know that your abbey is the only light that Christianity can oppose to the thirty-six libraries of Baghdad, to the ten thousand codices of the Vizir Ibn al-Alkami, that the number of your Bibles equals the two thousand four hundred Korans that are the pride of Cairo, and that the reality of your cases is luminous evidence against the proud legend of the infidels who years ago claimed (intimates as they are of the Prince of Falsehood) the library of Tripoli was rich in six million volumes and inhabited by eighty thousand commentators and two hundred scribes.[12]

But why should one not be able to visit such a wonder of European culture? The abbot's explanation sounds mysterious:

> "The library was laid out on a plan which has remained obscure to all over the centuries, and which none of the monks is called upon to know. Only the librarian has received the secret from the librarian who preceded him, and he communicates it, while still alive, to the assistant librarian, so that death will not take him by surprise and rob the community of that knowledge. And the secret seals the lips of both men. Only the librarian has, in addition to that knowledge, the right to move through the labyrinth of the books. . . .[13]

And, the abbot continues, "only the librarian knows, from the collocation of the volume, from its degree of inaccessibility, what secrets, what truths or falsehoods, the volume contains."[14] Later Jorge of Burgos, the library's blind guardian and its personified memory, will say, "The library is testimony to truth and to error."[15] And because it contains both, not only is its use subject to the strict control of its master, but also it is laid out in such a way that "the library defends itself, immeasurable as the truth it houses, deceitful as the falsehood it guards. A spiritual labyrinth, it is also a terrestrial labyrinth. You might enter and you might not emerge."[16]

The abbot leaves the curious detective for the time being with this warning. In their first attempt to get into the labyrinth, William and his young companion Adson have some unpleasant experiences. Not only do they have terrifying visions and hallucinations produced by distorting mirrors and poisonously glimmering oil lamps, but they are increasingly disconcerted by their loss of orientation in the bafflingly laid out passages. Only a lucky accident enables them to find their way out.

The only hope for a second attempt is a methodically worked-out reconstruction of the builder's plan. Only this promises to function as a successful thread of Ariadne: "We will use the mathematical sciences. . . . The library was built by a human mind that thought in a mathematical fashion, because without mathematics you cannot build labyrinths."[17] But the arrangement of the passages that lay in darkness corresponds to no mathematical law, and that makes the business even stickier. William cannot resist praising the labyrinth: "The maximum of confusion achieved with the maximum of order: it seems a sublime calculation. The builders of the library were great masters."[18]

The second exploratory mission into the interior of the labyrinth[19] is not only to complete the architectural plan of the library, which—as they deduce from inscriptions in the rooms—is "laid out and arranged according to the image of the terraqueous orb,"[20] but also to determine the subject matter and arrangement of the books in the rooms they have discovered. They leaf through the folios as if they were exploring "a mysterious continent or a terra incognita,"[21] for they are looking for the one and only book that it is important for them to find, the corpus delicti of all the crimes that followed the first death in the "abbey of horror."[22] They do locate the room they are looking for, the middle of the labyrinth, which is not, however, in the middle of the Aedificium, but in its south tower. It is called the *Finis Africae*. But they do not for the present find the way into it. When, in a later attempt, as a result of a lucky guess, they succeed in opening the secret door to the center, they find themselves confronting Jorge of Burgos, the blind seer, who shows them the sought-after book and reveals himself as the criminal.

The Library

When the labyrinthine self-defense of the library was no longer sufficient to hold off human curiosity, means of psychological terror had to be used in addition, and when even these failed, the librarian, convinced that he had "to defend the library tooth and nail,"[23] resorted to sophisticatedly concealed murder—ultimately solely to protect a single book from discovery.

Before we deal with this book, the secret motive of the eerie series of murders has to be discovered. In the end, behind all the psychology lies a piece of ideology. Or is it the other way around?

To young Father Benno from Uppsala, it seems incomprehensible to guard the treasures of a library like secrets, instead of making them available to researchers from all over the world, a view that corresponds to our enlightened scientific understanding, and Benno "considered that a monk-scholar had a right to know everything the library contained."[24] Of the monks, these "men who live among books, with books, from books,"[25] the narrator says:

> For these men devoted to writing, the library was at once the celestial Jerusalem and an underground world on the border between terra incognita and Hades. They were dominated by the library, by its promises and by its prohibitions. They lived with it, for it, and perhaps against it, sinfully hoping one day to violate all its secrets. Why should they not have risked death to satisfy a curiosity of their minds, or have killed to prevent someone from appropriating a jealously guarded secret of their own?[26]

Sinful pride, "intellectual pride," the pious narrator calls this temptation of knowledge.[27] By contrast, William regards the hunger for knowledge of the young bookworms initially with sympathy, but ultimately, clairvoyantly, he recognizes the hidden motive of their striving. When Benno eagerly becomes the assistant of the blind librarian so as to gain access for himself to the secret sources, William makes the following evaluation:

> Benno . . . is the victim of a great lust. . . . Like many scholars, he has a lust for knowledge. Knowledge for its own sake. Barred from a part of this knowledge, he

wanted to seize it. Now he has it. . . . Benno's (thirst for knowledge) is merely insatiable curiosity, intellectual pride, another way for a monk to transform and allay the desires of his loins, or the ardor that makes another man a warrior of the faith or of heresy.[28]

With this Freudian diagnosis, we seem to have arrived at the crux of the matter. The hidden mainspring behind the thirst for knowledge of a Benno of Uppsala is a driving will to power such as has been the shaping force behind modern science from the beginning. It is a sterile lust, because it feeds on and back into itself, a lust "that has nothing to do with love."[29]

Completely different and yet strangely akin is the outlook of Jorge of Burgos, for whom the sought-after end justified even the means of murder. He sees the mission of his order as the study and the preservation of knowledge, and preservation for him definitely does not mean searching for knowledge. What is there after all to search for? "There is no progress, no revolution of ages, in the history of knowledge, but at most a continuous and sublime recapitulation."[30] And he substantiates his view by calling upon the divine authority of the Bible: "I am He who is, said the God of the Jews. I am the way, the truth, and the life, said our Lord. There you have it: knowledge is nothing but the awed comment on these two truths."[31]

This is a medieval view of knowledge and science that seems long outmoded, yet it lies at the root of all fundamentalism, today as then. In order to assure the welfare of humanity, eternal or temporal, "the guardians who with the greatest kindness have taken it upon themselves to watch over them"[32] have limited the totality of all that is knowable—an intellectual labyrinth with many possible ways to go astray—to that which is unequivocal and easily digestible. It is exactly as though an artificial maze were constructed and equipped with sophisticated instruments of defense and intimidation in order to block off the vast realm of knowledge from those supposedly imperiled by it and in order to guarantee the discovery of truth only in accordance with the pattern of the classical labyrinth—providing a single way, free of intersections, not to be tread without effort, yet inevitably leading to the goal.

The Library

In the peripherally set center of the maze of the abbey library, Jorge of Burgos is preparing to eat the most secret of the forbidden books, to devour it so that it does not reach the eyes of the world, despite the fact that the sign reader, William, has already reconstructed the general outlines of it. It is the purportedly lost second book of Aristotle's *Poetics,* the greatest philosophical work on comedy and laughter.

Is that all? People underestimate the spirit of philosophy, particularly when it expresses itself in a work of aesthetics—Jorge knows this all too well. Every work of Aristotle that came to the knowledge of the pious scholars of the Middle Ages, he believes, "destroyed a part of that learning that Christianity had accumulated over the centuries."[33] But what might be expected to happen if everyday, plebeian laughter were raised to the level of an art by the supreme philosophical authority of the Occident, "defined as a new art, unknown even to Prometheus, for canceling fear"? "And," Jorge adds illuminatingly, "what would we be, we sinful creatures, without fear, perhaps the most foresighted, the most loving of the divine gifts?"[34] For the old librarian, the revelation of the philosophy of laughter would amount to a Satanic triumph, the conquest of "the dark powers of corporal matter." And yet for him, any means are acceptable, even the destruction of human life. Appalled, William responds, "You are the devil. . . . They lied to you. The Devil is not the Prince of Matter; the Devil is the arrogance of the spirit, faith without the smile, truth that is never seized by doubt."[35]

And then the concluding scene in the Aedificium. Jorge rips the damp pages of the book into thin strips and puts them into his mouth, and when William tries to get the book away from him, he runs from the room. In the ensuing scuffle, he knocks a lamp over onto a pile of books, which go up in a blaze of flame, as does, then, the whole marvelous library, the pride of Christendom.

The interest in Eco's novel continued all through the 1980s, as evinced by the millions of copies printed all over the world and the seemingly endless reviews, discussions, and interpretations it provoked. What the clever reader at least sensed, the professionals finally demonstrated through precise analysis: Eco's Middle Ages are a wonderful camouflage! The deviser of this camouflage, as well as his book, were characterized as intellectual chameleons.[36]

Even on superficial reflection we can see Sherlock Holmes peeping out from behind William of Baskerville. And it doesn't end there—his assistant Adso of Melk nearly has to be the not less well known Dr. Watson. And Jorge of Burgos, the blind librarian? It is scarcely to be believed that Eco's model for this sinister figure was his literary idol, the blind librarian Jorge Luis Borges of Buenos Aires! And by following Borges's tracks, we are led to the intellectual center of the monastic mystery novel. In one of his labyrinth stories, "The Library of Babel,"[37] he portrayed the world as a labyrinth of books:

> The universe (which others call the Library) is composed of a boundless and perhaps infinite number of hexagonal galleries, with broad ventilation shafts in the middle, which are surrounded by very low railings. From each hexagon one can see the storey below and the storey above—without end.[38]

The shelves of this "monstrously huge library" contain "all possible combinations of the twenty-some-odd orthographic signs (the number of which though extraordinarily large is still not infinite) along with everything that can be expressed by them in all languages."[39] This includes the totality of everything written and writable, but "for every comprehensible expression, there are miles of meaningless cacaphonies, linguistic junk, incoherent gibberish."[40]

In this mighty universe of books, the people of the Library are in the process of trying to find the one unique book that provides information on humanity's fundamental mysteries—the manner and time of the Library's origin.[41] That it was a god who created it is clear to the narrator:

> The human being, the imperfect librarian, might be the work of chance or of an evil demiurge; the universe, so elegantly fitted out with shelves, with enigmatic volumes, with inexhaustible stairs for the traveling librarian and toilets for the sedentary, can only be the work of a god.[42]

The Library

The notion that on one shelf in one of the hexagonal galleries there must be a book that is the "epitome and abstract of all of them" leads among the people to the superstition of "the man of the book," a librarian who has examined this book and therefore is like God.[43] That this enlightened person exists or at one time existed is also the uncertain hope of the narrator at the end of a long life of wandering through the labyrinth of "impenetrable books,"[44] books that are formless and chaotic in character. He concludes his reflections on the nature of the Library with the following words:

> I am so bold as to consider proposing the following solution for the age-old problem: *The Library is limitless and cyclical.* If an eternal traveler were to cross it in any given direction, after centuries he would discover that the same volumes reappeared in the same disorder (which, repeated, would become an order—*the* order). In my solitude I rejoice in this elegant hope.[45]

The Library of Babel is a vertical maze, whose corresponding horizontal counterpart we find in another of the master's tales, "The Garden of Branching Paths."[46] In the course of the story, this reveals itself as "the work of the all but undisentangleable Ts'ui Pen"[47] and as a chaotic novel whose principle of organization is branching in time. However, the key word "time" is not mentioned a single time. For Ts'ui Pen, this book, is "though an incomplete one, not a false image of the cosmic totality":[48]

> He believed in unending time series, a growing, vertigo-provoking network of times moving in the same direction tending away from and towards each other. This web pattern composed of times—approaching one another, branching, intersecting or for centuries knowing nothing of one another—encompasses all possibilities.[49]

From Jorge Luis Borges, a direct path runs to the zeitgeist phenomenon of the 1980s known to the general public as postmodernism.[50] In his novel *Name of the Rose,* Umberto Eco created in the character William of Baskerville an attractive and likeable advocate of this outlook, a literary embodiment not only of the medieval philosopher William of Ockham, but also of the bright side of the eccentric literato, Jorge Luis Borges.

> In the prologue of the novel, Adso says of his admired master William that he was moved . . . solely by the desire for truth, and by the suspicion—which I could see he always harbored—that the truth was not what was appearing to him at any given moment.[51]

This is a clear message—he never degenerated to the point of holding the view that a person can appropriate truth as a possession. Nonetheless, at the end, as the labyrinth of the library is being destroyed forever by the flames, he has to admit, "I behaved stubbornly, pursuing a semblance of order, when I should have known well that there is no order in the universe."[52] The acumen of the sign-reading sleuth is no match for the labyrinthine interconnectedness of the signs, no matter how good he is at dealing with them one at a time.

His laborious process of conjecture seemingly proceeds in the labyrinth of the action of the novel in accordance with the common procedure of trial and error,[53] however, the world as a whole that William is thinking about in his last conversation with Adso, is an immense maze, a "garden of branching paths," the "vertigo-provoking network" of Ts'ui Pen. Such a network has been expressed by the metaphor of a rhizome, as "a confusion of nodules and knots."[54]

> The world has become chaotic, but the book remains the image of the world, the rootlet of the chaosmos instead of the root of the cosmos.[55]

Thus in the epilogue to his novel, Umberto Eco speaks of the rhizome labyrinth:

> The rhizome labyrinth is so multidimensionally interwoven, that every passage can immediately connect with every other. It has neither a center nor a periphery, and also no exit, since it is potentially endless.[56]

Whoever in the face of a reality like this makes the totalitarian claim of being in possession of the only right and salutary interpretation of the world must, in the medieval world of William of Baskerville, bear the features of the Antichrist:

> "The Antichrist can be born from piety itself, from excessive love of God or of the truth, as the heretic is born from the saint and the possessed from the seer. Fear prophets, Adso, and those prepared to die for the truth. . . . Perhaps the mission of those who love mankind is to make people laugh at the truth, *to make the truth laugh,* because the only truth lies in learning to free ourselves from the insane passion for the truth."[57]

Whether or not this solves the problem of truth is beside the point. In any case, humility is indicated. What is left in the end is what Adso as an old man discovers decades later in the rubble of the once awe-inspiring abbey, that "mirror of the world," and what he laboriously reassembles—fragments, pitiful vestiges of the wondrous library:[58]

> At the end of my patient reconstruction, I had before me a kind of lesser library, a symbol of the greater, vanished one: a library made up of fragments, quotations, unfinished sentences, amputated stumps of books.[59]

ELEVEN

Prison

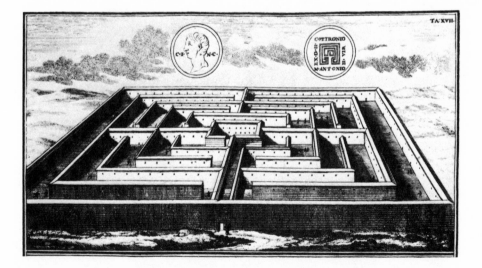

Reconstruction of the Cretan Labyrinth as a prison,
by Johann Bernhard Fischer von Erlach (1656–1723).

The labyrinth has a crookedly hung gate,
Difficult of access:
How far you have to go
To rush in from outside
Leads you that much further again
Through the narrowly winding wandering ways
Inward from the point of the exit.
With its outward-leading passages it spellbinds
you day after day,
And its twists and turns play their
contemptuous game with you,
Like a dream with its empty faces;
Until Master Chronos melts away,
And, oh, doer of darkness Death receives you,
And not a chance is left you of reaching the exit.

—FROM A MEDIEVAL LABYRINTH POEM

It is not far from "postmodern modernism" to "catastrophic modernism."[1] Around the time of the Orwellian year of terror, 1984, the sense of crisis that had been building since the miserable end of the optimistic upheaval of the sixties came to a head:

> The Apocalypse is at hand. We monsters have known it for a long time, and we all know it. Behind the party factionalism, the armament and disarmament debates, the military parades, and the antiwar marches, behind the facade of pacifism and the endless peace treaties, there is a secret accord, a great unspoken mutual understanding—that we have to put an end to ourselves and those like us, as soon and as thoroughly as possible, without mercy, without scruple, and without any survivors.[2]

Those are the terms in which Ulrich Horstmann expresses himself in his timely manifesto *Philosophie der Menschenflucht* (The Philosophy of the Flight from Humanity), which is dedicated to the "monster" who does not deserve to be called a human being.

The *vanitas* mood of the Baroque period ("all is vanity") has returned with a vengeance, and as if this needed special confirmation in Germany, Robert Burton's *Anatomy of Melancholy,* from the year 1621, appeared for the first time in German translation, put out by the above-named exponent of "anthropofugal" thinking.

The newly formulated subtitle of the old book shows what sort of an attitude one is supposed to take toward it: "On the Ubiquity of Melancholy, Its Causes and Symptoms, as well as the Art of Enduring It." And in the text we read:

> We lead a contentious, morose, disorderly, melancholy and miserable life; and if we could foresee what is to come, and if we had a choice, we would rather reject this miserable existence than accept it. In short, the world itself is a maze, a labyrinth of errors, a desert, a wilderness, a bandits' cave, strewn with fetid meres and horrid rocks, full of abysses, a heavy yoke, an ocean of misery in which crime and misfortune wash over each other or chase each other like waves.[3]

Though playing the old song one more time, late modernism developed its own variations of the well-known melody, and that considerably in advance of the ominous year, 1984.

To desert and wilderness, Comenius and Gracián preferred the big city as a cipher of the labyrinthine quality; nor has this Babel of confusion[4] fallen into oblivion in the present century either. Michel Butor's 1956 novel, *The Schedule,* proves it.[5] However, the conception we find here is not typical of its time. Instead here the labyrinth is reduced once again to its Daedalic form—it is concentrated in a single edifice; whether this is upon the earth or in its depths does not seem essential for the moment.

While the philosophically motivated truth seekers, following the literary tracks of Jorge Luis Borges, were making their journey into the labyrinthine Library, the pragmatic representatives of the no longer at all gay science were barricading themselves in ostensibly completely unlabyrinthine edifices—for example, in the "comfortable if dilapidated villa of the private sanatorium, 'Les Cerisiers,' " the scene of the comedy *The Physicists* by Friedrich Dürrenmatt, an institution that turns out to be an insane asylum and even worse: a closely guarded prison from which there is no escape.[6]

In accordance with good sense, libraries and insane asylums are built on the surface of the earth, even if they are to be escape proof. A labyrinth, however, that is completely without exit, a kind of super prison, would logically find its place in the underworld.

Marie Luise Kaschnitz envisioned such a cavern world of no escape when, in 1955, she conceived of a game "the theme of which is Theseus's adventure in the Labyrinth:"[7] A young married couple is singled out from a group of tourists who are sightseeing in a subterranean labyrinth; the couple has experienced the underground reality of the modern world "in the form of a gigantic Luna Park":

> The modern labyrinth is a pandemonium of noises, which are no more than an intensification of those of modern traffic and factory work. In the up-to-date labyrinth, there is a superhighway on which real blood flows, a shooting arcade in which living people are shot at, a monster who appears in the form of an unpretentious bank clerk. Theseus experiences the thrill of excessive speed, the seduction of vice, and the urge to kill.[8]

In the past, Ariadne was able to counter the urge toward doom and destruction successfully:

> The girl Ariadne, who in the course of the millennia has continued again and again to rescue young men from the errant ways of their youth and who has always been abandoned by them, is now here again, filled with the old confidence and hope. But the age-old seduction doesn't work on the new Theseus. He is not interested in happiness, nor in returning home; what he wants is

to plumb the experience of the Labyrinth, which he perceives as a radical intensification of real life, to the very depths. He doesn't believe in love as a force of redemption and is a stranger to nature.[9]

In this situation the highest experience the *joie de vivre* can aim at is "to set in movement the lever of total annihilation." But before Theseus can do this, "the lever begins to move all by itself."[10] It is left open "whether this annihilation is thus effected or whether the mysterious power only destroys the nefarious forces of the Labyrinth, thus helping humanity toward a new, more meaningful life."[11]

The imprisonment seems to be a double one. Theseus is shut up in a consciousness that finds the peak experience of life in the thrill of progress, no matter whether it is in heaven or in a hell on earth.[12] In addition to this, the process of the world has now moved completely beyond the reach of subjective demands and objections. Progress, as ominous as it might be, has achieved autonomy. The future has been denatured into "an inalterably fixed continuum of so-called material determinants," into "a 'repository of bondage' (Max Weber)."[13] The lever moves by itself, the human act seems to have become superfluous. How could Ariadne intervene here? That she should share Theseus's destiny, as the plan provides, is ultimately not the wish of the author either. In any case, her plan never became a literary reality.

Things seem to have gone pretty much the same with an enterprise of Friedrich Dürrenmatt, "a matter devoid of action," of which the author says it was "really an endless nightmare" for him.[14] This is the unwritten story "from the papers of a custodian," arising out of experiences and insights connected with the Second World War, condensed to the simile of a "world of meaninglessness," the image of a "cosmic labyrinth."[15] The story remained a forgotten fragment, but in the postwar years, under the influence of the prevailing apocalyptic mood, it took on final form, and received the title *Der Winterkrieg in Tibet* (The Winter War in Tibet).[16]

Awkwardly, but still in a manner comprehensible for every-

Friedrich Dürrenmatt, *Labyrinth III* (1975).

Prison

one, the narrator defines his task in the world following the Third World War:

> I am a mercenary and proud of it. I fight against the enemy not only in the name of the Administration, but also as an instrument, if only a humble one, of the accomplishment of its task, that is, of the part of its task that obliges it to fight against the enemy; for it is not only there to help the citizens but also to protect them. I am a fighter in the Winter War in Tibet.[17]

The surface of the earth has been laid waste, and life in old Europe has been nearly wiped out. However, the fight for the cause of the Administration continues under the earth—in a labyrinth of shafts and passages "that are interconnected with one another and constitute an unmappable system of veins in the mighty massif, so that there too the hostile parties encounter each other by surprise and butcher each other."[18]

Dürrenmatt's Theseus[19] fights with an unknown Minotaur:

> The question of the enemy is not something a mercenary can allow to come up, for the simple reason that it will kill him. If the enemy becomes a question in his mind, even if only unconsciously, he cannot fight. . . . It is of no interest to him who the enemy is, what he is fighting for, or who is in command.[20]

That sounds spirited, the way a soldier should talk. But behind this convincing voice is hidden a Theseus such as no one has ever encountered:

> Legless, I sit in my wheelchair in the old cave. My hands too are gone. My left arm extends seamlessly into a machine pistol. I fire on anyone who comes into my line of sight. The tunnels are strewn with corpses. Fortunately, there are rats. My right hand is an all-purpose set of tools: pliers, hammer, screwdriver, shears, a stylus, etc., all made of steel.[21]

In the meantime, fortunately, it has become quiet in the labyrinth. A pause in the fighting? Theseus makes use of his leisure time

139

to scratch his thoughts onto the rock walls, covering the walls of
the cave with inscriptions, "which have no other purpose but to
depict the nature of the Administration—in which the administra-
tor and those administrated can no longer be distinguished."[22]

How long he has led this subterranean existence, he does not
know, but he senses that he is, for a great distance all around, "the
only defender of the Administration."[23] One day, as he is following
a glimmer of light, he discovers an exhibition hall where wax figures depict scenes in the Winter War. The supposed reality has
become a legend, an attraction for tourists. Terrified and confused,
he looks for a new hideaway, encounters an eerie double, and falls
down a shaft.

> Clearly I am in a cave. I feel that my face is a bloody
> mass. The floor is a rubble of stones. I drag myself labo-
> riously along the wall. The cave must be boundless.
> Sometimes the draught is icy, sometimes an unbearable
> heat take over. Probably the huge workshops where they
> make the weapons are nearby. Whether they are ours or
> those of the enemy I don't know. My situation is hope-
> less. But now thrown back entirely on myself, creeping
> along the wall of the immense cave, which often twists
> and turns in the strangest way, I can ask myself the ques-
> tion that I never permitted myself during the fighting:
> Who is the enemy? The question can no longer disable
> me, nor the answer either. I no longer have anything to
> lose. That is my strength. I have become unconquerable.
> I have solved the riddle of the Winter War. . . .[24]

Theseus and the Minotaur have become one, each the mirror
image of the other. Or in the words of the mercenary: "The goal of
the human being is to be his own enemy—man and his shadow
are one. The world falls to whoever grasps this truth; he gives the
Administration back its meaning."[25]

The figure of the Minotaur already occupied Dürrenmatt in
his ink drawings before the completion of the first part of his *Stoffe*
(Matters). In his notes to these, he wrote:

> A part of the Labyrinth is the Minotaur. He is a freak
> and as such he is the image of the individual, the isolated

Friedrich Dürrenmatt, illustration from *The Minotaur*.

individual. The individual faces a world which for him
is inscrutable. The Labyrinth is the world seen from the
point of view of the Minotaur. Thus the Minotaur pages
show the Minotaur as without the experience of the
other, of a you. All he understands is to rape and to kill.
It is not because of Theseus that he dies. He dies like one
of so-and-so-many heads of cattle.[26]

This characterization is dead on for the figure of the mercenary in *Winterkrieg*, for the Theseus who has to recognize himself
as the Minotaur. A variation of this is found in the 1985 story
"Minotaurus: Eine Ballade" (The Minotaur: A Ballad), with drawings by the author.[27]

In the labyrinthine closet of mirrors—shades of Leonardo's
invention!—the misshapen creature cringes not only from his own
mirror reflection, but also from the mirror reflections of his mirror
reflection: "He found himself in a world of cringing beings, with-

out realizing that the being was himself."[28] Experimenting childishly with his likenesses, he finally concludes that he is one among many, and "he danced like a child, he danced like a monstrous father of himself. . . ."[29]

Only when other beings appear—the sacrificial victims meant for him, beings who are not dancing—does the Minotaur grasp that there is something besides Minotaurs. A young woman is the first one he discovers. Playfully, he takes her, rapes her, and kills her involuntarily. The others, he tears to pieces, full of hatred, when one of the young men wounds him. Possessed with hatred, he then turns on his mirror image, smashes the glass walls in order to destroy it, and only slowly grasps that it is himself he is attacking.

> He tried to run away, but no matter where he turned, he was always face to face with himself. He was walled in by himself, all over was himself, himself was endless, reflected by the Labyrinth into infinity. He sensed that there were not many Minotaurs, but only one Minotaur, that there was only one being like him, never one before him, none after him, that he was the only one, simultaneously shut out and shut in. . . .[30]

When he wakes up the next morning, he is astonished to find himself face to face with another Minotaur, not his mirror reflection, but the unconsciously longed-for Other. He shouts with joy, "with joy that he was no longer isolated, no longer simultaneously shut in and shut out, that there was a second Minotaur, not only an 'I' but also a 'you.'[31] As he falls into the arms of the other one, "trusting that he had found a friend,"[32] the other one stabs him— Theseus has deceived him with the mask of the bull man. In one of his last interviews, Dürrenmatt gave this frightening résumé:

> The Minotaur can only be killed by this large trick image of a Minotaur, just by Theseus who wears the mask and deceives the Minotaur. The individual finds his friend in the other who looks like himself. And in making him his friend, he finds his death.[33]

A confusing message. Is this a statement about the essence of man, who is a wolf for other men—the law that underlies the Administration[34]—or is it a poetically enciphered diagnosis of modern industrial society?

German Sociologists like Ulrich Beck prefer the empirical alternative. They speak of individualization and define it in a threefold manner as a release from traditional relationships of power and supply; as a loss of traditional securities, which amounts to a demystification and desacralization of consciousness; and finally—a seeming paradox—as a new kind of social bonding, which expresses itself in the standardization of the freed individual.[35] The result of this process is an individualized mass public or "the standardized collective existence of isolated mass hermits,"[36] a phenomenon fraught with contradictions, which Günther Anders saw, just the other way around, in terms of the "antiquatedness of the individual."[37]

What for some time already has been a commonplace in North America is now setting in after the proverbial time lag on the European continent—after all the other things, now this too: "a society of growing speechlessness, increasing isolation, loneliness, lack of relationship," in which people are never alone, "because through their cable-equipped living rooms and their electronically networked workplaces, they live always as part of the mass."[38] Moreover, the life of the individual who has been separated from his old ties and securities is increasingly determined by a new "system of care-providing, administrative, and political institutions,"[39] with the result that private matters and political ones mingle and overlap in the most problematic possible fashion. "In a certain manner," suggests Ulrich Beck, "what arises are Kafkas in mass quantities, in the sense of Kafka characters, banal characters in a realistic novel who know they are moving in a medium of paradoxes as fish move in water."[40]

The Minotaur in the Labyrinth—is this today's "single" stylized into a mythological figure, enclosed in the closet of mirrors of his "self-development," provided by a welfare-oriented "administration" with ever new means of consumption, who is unable to escape from his prison because the trap has become so perfect? I couldn't say for sure. But must not Dürrenmatt have had Kafka in mind in all of this, the "poet of the labyrinth,"[41] the involuntary prophet of our neurotic century, this same Kafka who inspired our sociological informant above?

One of Kafka's last stories, written at the end of 1923, is a peculiar document in the labyrinth genre. This is "The Burrow,"[42] an image of the author's own life and a vision of the society of our day. Here too the Minotaur is alone, but he speaks to us:

> I have completed the construction of my burrow and it seems to be successful. . . . It is secured as safely as anything in this world can be secured. . . . When autumn sets in, to possess a burrow like mine, and a roof over your head, is great good fortune for anyone getting on in years. Every hundred yards I have widened the passages into little round cells; there I can curl myself up in comfort and lie warm. There I sleep the sweet sleep of tranquility, of satisfied desire, of achieved ambition; for I possess a house.[43]

The animal, which resembles a badger, is the "sole master of all the manifold passages and rooms" in a subterranean burrow, which for security, boasts an entrance labyrinth, "a whole little maze of passages,"[44] and also as a whole represents a kind of super labyrinth. Not quite in the middle lies the main cell, which he proudly calls the Castle Keep:

> In the Castle Keep I assemble my stores; everything over and above my daily wants that I capture inside the burrow, and everything I bring back with me from my hunting expeditions outside, I pile up here. The place is so spacious that food for half a year scarcely fills it. Consequently I can divide up my stores, walk about among them, play with them, enjoy their plenty and their various smells, and reckon up exactly how much they represent. That done, I can always arrange accordingly, and make my calculations and hunting plans for the future, taking into account the season of the year.[45]

The Kafkan Minotaur has every reason to be content: "Your house is protected and self-sufficient. You live in peace, warm, well nourished. . . ."[46] And yet he is filled with deepest malaise. In his head, a thought labyrinth is steadily being built and indestructibly solidified: "I live in peace in the inmost chamber of my house, and meanwhile the enemy may be burrowing his way slowly and stealthily straight toward me. . . . And it is not only by external enemies that I am threatened. There are also enemies in the bowels of the earth."[47] Since this fear was awakened in him, he has "scarcely had one full minute of peace." It is true, he has never seen the supposed enemies, but there are legends that tell of them. And so, filled with anxiety, he is constantly occupied with perfecting his defense measures and securing his stores by redistributing them to auxiliary storage rooms. The entrance labyrinth is no longer adequate for his heightened security needs:

> And if a serious attack were attempted, what pattern of entrance at all would be likely to save me? An entrance can deceive, can lead astray, can give the attacker no end of worry, and the present one too can do that at a pinch. But a really serious attack has to be met by an instantaneous mobilization of all the resources in the burrow and all the forces of my body and soul—that is evident.[48]

The animal longs for the happy days when he could still believe that "the strength of the burrow had raised me above the destructive struggle of former times."[49] It becomes clear to him that this is no mere security shelter but "my castle, which can never belong to anyone else,"[50] which belongs to him to such a degree that he is one with its passages and rooms: "You belong to me, I to you, we are united."[51] No doubt about it, if worse came to worse, he would perish with them!

But it doesn't come to this. The story, though supposedly finished at one point,[52] remains a fragment. Is the end left open? The fearful anxiety becomes more and more heightened. The animal tunes his hearing to the stillness of the burrow in order to pick up a trace of the foe. Every noise intensifies his fear. Finally, he hears "a faint whistling, audible only at long intervals, a mere nothing to which I don't say that one could actually get used. . . ."[53] All attempts to calm himself fail: "My imagination will not rest, and I have actually come to believe—it is useless to deny it to myself—

145

that the whistling is made by some beast, and moreover not by a great many small ones, but by a single big one."[54]

Fatefully identified with the comfort of the burrow that has become so peculiarly his own, shut up in the prison of his fear, the Minotaur looks toward an uncertain future.

TWELVE

Daedalus and Icarus

Daedalus and Icarus flee from the Labyrinth. Limestone relief by
an unknown artist (probably seventeenth century),
Compiègne, France.

In my view there is no prison to deter an obstinate
prisoner seeking to escape, no gate and no moat that
boldness and resolve could not pass.
—ANDRÉ GIDE, *Theseus*

Escape from the prison!

The Athenian-inspired story of the Cretan Labyrinth does not end with the death of the Minotaur and the carrying off of Princess Ariadne. We still have Minos, the defeated king, betrayed and despondent. His mind is taken up with revenge, and his wrath is bent on the author of all his misfortunes, Daedalus.

Too late Minos learned that the Athenian emigré had not only been his savior in time of need, when Pasiphae brought the ghastly miscreation into the world, but had also played a key role in its coming into being. Or is this rather simply knowledge he had long repressed? In any case Daedalus was not only the ingenious architect of the Labyrinth, but also the maker of the accursed love machine, the prosthetic cow. And for that he had to pay! Punishing Pasiphae was out of the question; rather, what was in the king's mind was clan responsibility, extending the guilt of Pasiphae's helper to the other males in his family. This meant Icarus, Daedalus's son through his relationship with Naucrate, one of the female slaves at the royal court, was also to be arrested, imprisoned along with his father—where else? (oh, irony of fate)—in the Labyrinth, the state prison which had just been deprived of its function. So now there they sat, guarded by teams from the Minoan state security service; or else they wandered, without benefit of a guiding thread, through the endless passages, hither and yon, down a story into the underground in one place, up a story again in another. It is told that Pasiphae made use of her connections and secretly arranged for the two of them to escape, but a more fascinating story is the one in which Daedalus devised the means for the escape from

148

the Labyrinth himself through one last triumph of his inventive gift.

The Labyrinth was by no means an entirely enclosed structure, as one might expect, but was open on top. In constructing it, Daedalus presumed he could depend on it not being given to human beings to travel like birds or gods in the lofty heights. The dimension measured out to man is the horizontal, not the vertical. In taking it upon himself to construct a technical means of flying in the air, Daedalus not only became the progenitor of modern air travel, but also a rebel against the limited conditions of human existence, against the purely horizontal dimensionality of life. Feathers of all kinds, large and small, were required for his grandiose project, and that is where I think Pasiphae's friends might have helped him. He fixed the large feathers with threads and the small ones with wax into two masterfully crafted pairs of wings—one pair for Icarus, the other for himself.

When the time for the escape came—the test flights had already been successfully concluded—the father, with tears in his eyes, urgently warned his beloved son: "Be warned, my son! Do not fly too high, for otherwise the sun will melt the wax; and do not sink down too low, for otherwise the feathers will be dampened by the sea!"[1] With wings on their backs they set out, and as they left the labyrinthine prison behind them, the father once more gave his warning, crying out with fearful concern, "Follow close behind me, and don't change direction!" Beating their wings, they moved off to the northeast. Fishermen, sheepherders, and farmers stared after them in astonishment, filled with pious awe at the sight of the supposed divine beings.

To begin with, everything went according to plan. However, then, after having left Naxos, Delos, and Paros behind, Icarus refused to continue following his father, and filled with joy by the strength of his wings, flew higher and higher—and closer to the sun. When Daedalus looked back over his shoulder, Icarus had disappeared. Ovid describes this catastrophe movingly in his *Metamorphoses:*

> The nearness of the consuming sun made soft the fragrant wax, the feathers' fastener. The wax melted away.

He stroked with naked arms, but with no wings, he
could beat no air, and the mouth, still crying out his
father's name, was swallowed up by the blue waters. . . .
And the father, now a father no longer, shouted,
"Icarus! Icarus! Where are you? Under which stretch of
heaven shall I look for you?"[2]

When at last he spotted the feathers in the waves, he flew around
and around until he found his son's corpse. Cursing his craftsman-
ship, he bore the body to a nearby island and buried it there.

For Daedalus this was the moment of truth. His thoughts returned to his native Athens. There, as a celebrated artist and engi-
neer, he had had a young person like Icarus confided to his
care—Talos, the son of his sister, Polycaste. The bright lad had
been a receptive student, and thus it happened that, when he was
only twelve years old, he had surpassed his master in skill. The
saw, the potter's wheel, and the compass had been his brilliant
inventions. For a time Daedalus had succeeded in giving out these
inventions of his protegé as his own, but the people of Athens were
not ones to let the wool be pulled over their eyes for long. Spoiled
by his successes, Daedalus was overcome by unbearable envy. One
day he took Talos with him up onto the roof of the Temple of
Athens, the Acropolis, supposedly to share the splendid vista with
him, and pushed the guileless youth to his death. The murder was
discovered, but Daedalus evaded the trial by fleeing to Crete. From
then on, everything he devised or invented resulted in disaster,
lastly, his great invention of a mechanism for human flight. Was it
that Icarus wanted to surpass him as Talos actually had? Emotions
had turned the coolly planned, painstakingly organized escape venture into a fiasco—inappropriate emotions! Boldness and resolve
overcome any prison, when they are put to work in a realistic fashion. Anything that transgresses those bounds is ruinous! As Daedalus knew, Icarus had always been a dreamer; he had often
reproached his son for his mystic bent. Can one escape the Labyrinth of Minos when one has a labyrinth in one's own head, a
labyrinth of metaphysical illusions and Utopian wishful thinking,
of "fantasies, visions, or speculations without constancy, logic, or
solidity"?[3] You only survive if you have a cool head! Revolutions

against paternal authority and joyrides to the sun should be reserved for vacation time. Yes, that was it! Daedalus was now getting his bearings back fast. He should have foreseen this!

The now lonely man swung again into the air, flew further to the west and landed in Cumae, not far from Naples, in a place where the earth heaves up, taking the form of the gigantic grottos that form the entrance to Hades. In this place, he consecrated his wings to the god Apollo and built a temple to him with a golden roof and golden gates, which he decorated with commemorative images. On one of the double doors he depicted the death of Androgeos, Minos's son, and on the other the Cretan Labyrinth and his own fateful story. But his artistic powers failed him when it came to trying to capture in images the death of his son:

> In that high sculpture you, too, would have had
> Your great part, Icarus, had grief allowed.
> Twice your father had tried to shape your fall
> In gold, but twice his hands dropped.[4]

The next station on the way of the restless emigré was Kamikos in Sicily. King Cocalus received him with hospitality, and there too Daedalus was able to make himself useful by building buildings and creating fashionable pieces of jewelry for the daughter of the king.

In the meantime, Minos had been searching for the escapee. With his fleet, he sailed from city to city, and everywhere he went he showed a snail shell, saying that whoever was able to draw a threat through its twists and turns would receive a large reward. When he arrived in Kamikos, he also placed this same shell in the hands of his fellow king, Cocalus. The latter promised him the solution to the problem, and went in secret to Daedalus to get his advice. A knowing smile played over the features of the old master. He bored a hole in the tip of the snail shell, tied a silken thread to an ant, and induced it to crawl in through the hole. By spreading honey on the edges of the large main opening, he lured the insect on the thread through the spiral passages. Cocalus triumphantly returned the shell with the thread drawn through it and demanded the reward. However, Minos replied that only Daedalus could have found the solution, and insisted that his quarry be delivered into his hands. Or maybe the matter was handled in a somewhat more obliging fashion. In a friendly manner he asked Cocalus to let him have his old friend back. Soon a mutual agreement was reached. The day of departure was to be celebrated with a festive meal. But the Sicilian king's daughter was against Daedalus's departure. She did not want to have to give up the inventive art of the esteemed master, thus she hatched a ghastly plan. As Minos was taking a bath before the farewell banquet, she came to him and served him. But instead of pouring water over him, she doused him with boiling pitch.

Other sources purport to be more in the know about the details. According to them, Daedalus ran a pipe through the roof of the bath chamber, through which the princess ran boiling water into the bath. In the end Cocalus handed over the king's body to the Cretans with the disdainful explanation that Minos had tripped on a carpet and fallen into a cauldron of boiling water. A horrid and ignominious end for the great king! The king's followers, however, buried their dead ruler with great honor in the center of the Temple of Aphrodite on Kamikos. And Zeus appointed his son as one of the three judges of the dead in the underworld.

Daedalus's traces disappear in the darkness of myth. Is he perhaps still in action, that restless emigré and disaster-breeding "creator of ingenious artificialities, who cursed his own art?"[5]

Escaping from prison without getting into a fresh calamity— this was a problem that both Daedalus and Icarus were obviously incapable of solving. The father, it is true, saved his own life, but at the price of his future. He continued his production of incomparably clever and at the same time disastrous inventions at random, letting the chips fall where they would. What he was lacking he would surely not learn in old age. And Icarus? Could he have been saved from his disastrous fall and prepared properly for life?

Highly differing opinions exist on this point.[6] On the threshold of the modern age, Sebastian Brant rhymed in his *Narrenschiff* (Ship of Fools):

> Each day we see the foolish fall
> And scorn is heaped upon them all.

Daedalus and Icarus

Pieter Brueghel, *Landscape with the Fall of Icarus.*

They are scoffed at by the clever,
Who barely keep themselves together.
Had Phaeton never crossed the sky,
Icarus had never flown so high.
If both had heeded father's word,
Death and pain had not occurred.[7]

Icarus, a fool because he despised his father's authority, earned for himself the contempt of posterity. He could even, with a pious shudder, be identified with Satan, whose rebellion against God ended with the fall into hell, as we read in Milton's *Paradise Lost*.[8]

We see another point of view concerning Icarus's fate, which could be called a modern one, in a painting by Pieter Brueghel, his "Landscape with the Fall of Icarus."[9] This painting did not come to light until 1912—as though it had been biding its time through the centuries, awaiting the beginning of the twentieth to convey its pessimistic message.

In this picture the busy world ignores the young ascendant to heaven completely. Fishermen, sheepherders, and farmers do stare up in astonishment to wonder at a superhuman drama, as they did in the earlier tale, but remain occupied with their own concerns. Irritated, a person looking at the picture hunts for the falling youth. Icarus seems not to be there at all. Only after close inspection does the onlooker discover two legs sticking out of the sea in the lower right hand corner, and above them, floating in the air, a few feathers. Marie Luise Kaschnitz comments as follows: "Of the fall from heaven, the learned and sensible Brueghel records only the last moment, just those ludicrously flailing legs, as though he wanted to mock the pitiful end of a dream."[10]

W. H. Auden saw the whole resignation of our century with regard to youthful enthusiasms in Brueghel's image:

> About suffering they were never wrong,
> The Old Masters: how well they understood
> Its human position; how it takes place
> While someone else is eating or opening a window or just
>   walking dully along;
> . . . .
>
> In Brueghel's *Icarus,* for instance: how everything turns away
> Quite leisurely from the disaster; the ploughman may
> Have heard the splash, the forsaken cry,
> But for him it was not an important failure; the sun shone
> As it had to on the white legs disappearing into the green
> Water; and the expensive delicate ship that must have seen
> Something amazing, a boy falling out of the sky,
> Had somewhere to get to and sailed calmly on.[11]

But nevertheless—who else but Icarus could successfully escape the Labyrinth and win the future? Learning to fly is not enough. The father's appeals to his son's reason did not prevent the fateful flight into the heights, but a feeble low flight would have had no better result. What was Icarus, the bearer of our hopes, lacking? A sense of reality without a doubt! But should we wish that he had followed his father?

The attentive reader of the post-Labyrinthine tales will certainly not have failed to notice that the whole story is played out among men. The men have divested themselves of Pasiphae. Naucrate, the mother of Icarus, is no more than a genealogical memory. But what would Theseus have been without Ariadne? And what is Icarus without a helpful goddess, without a human Aphrodite?

It is not an abstract appeal to reason that Icarus needs, nor repetitive reminders of moral duties and obligations, but rather the power of eros, vibrations of love that do not carry him off into the infinite, but lead him into responsibility for the here and now and the future.

Ariadne Aphrodite, goddess of love and of life, manifest yourself anew!

Postscript

One shouldn't let oneself be carried away into histrionics by way of conclusion, and above all, one shouldn't resort to desperate prayers.

The bad consequences didn't take long to ripen. One of my daughters took a more intensive interest in her father's manuscript than anticipated, and was stopped by the concluding imperative invocation. "Who is this Ariadne Aphrodite who's supposed to show up at this point?" she wanted to know. This is exactly the kind of sixty-four-thousand-dollar question I would have liked to avoid. But such a daughterly inquiry is not to be eluded, and so I must at least essay an answer.

Let me say to avoid any misunderstandings that I am expecting neither the revelation of some neo-pagan mother goddess nor the appearance of a fundamentalistically renovated Madonna. I also set no store in the establishment of a feministic myth for the twenty-first century, being given the ludicrous and gruesome outcome of the heroic myth of the twentieth century. Before new Utopias are projected, I am hoping for the fulfillment of the oh-so-promising pledges made by our own century at a time when it was still young, and indeed, without the repetition of already committed mistakes.

A new society and a new culture were supposed to develop, the prophets of progressive enlightenment said in those days. They spoke as well, for example, of a new relationship between the sexes. Male dominance was to give way to a holistic human culture in which the values and right of women had their full place. The fulfillment of some of these youthful dreams of our century would be very helpful as it now draws to a close.

As far as Icarus is concerned, he has long had a need of a

female partner who could teach him the love of the earth and its creatures, dissuade him from technological omnipotence fantasies and masculine military games as well as from false mysticism, who could seduce him into the straightforward and basic service of life. Confidence characterizes such a woman; she has the savoir-faire of Ariadne and Aphrodite's charm.

It goes without saying that this new Ariadne can only perform these vitally essential services for Icarus if he is ready to discover in her his own self's other and to actualize in himself what he discovers.

Ariadne has many names. She is also called Sophia, wisdom. She is the companion that the Hebrew God Yahveh needs as much as the Greek Zeus and Roman Jupiter do; but she is most especially needed by the vainglorious *homo faber,* who often seems to have been abandoned by all good spirits.

The answer to my daughter seems to be something like that. I must just add that neither Daedalus nor Icarus escaped from the Labyrinth by getting themselves airborne through technical sophistication. It is true that the Labyrinth is open to the sky, but it still makes it necessary for us painstakingly to find our way on the ground, in the horizontal dimension. We escape from prison through our own effort, yet only by working with others. Together we have to work through our labyrinthine situation in a productive manner, rather than looking up into the sky with passive resignation or catapulting ourselves into the heavens.

So who is this Ariadne Aphrodite who's supposed to show up at this point? Quite simply, I say to my daughter, you have to find her in yourself! Then you can celebrate your marriage to Icarus, though I don't say it necessarily has to be a sacred one!

Notes

Despite intensive research it has not been possible in every case for the publishing house to locate the exact sources or copyright holders of texts and illustrations. The following listing is therefore not without gaps. We would be grateful for any relevant information. We should like to take this opportunity to express our thanks to the photographers and publishers for kindly granting permission to reproduce material controlled by them.

Introduction

1. Cf. Stanislaw Lem, *Die Ratte im Labyrinth* (The Rat in the Maze).
2. Gustav René Hocke's work first appeared as double volume 50/51 in the *RDE* in 1957. Rowolt published a new edition in 1987.
3. G. R. Hocke, *Die Welt als Labyrinth* (Hamburg, 1957), p. 99.
4. Hermann Pongs, *Franz Kafka: Dichter des Labyrinths* (Franz Kafka: Poet of the Labyrinth) (Heidelberg, 1960).
5. Marianne Thalmann, *Romantik und Manierismus* (Romanticism and Mannerism) (Stuttgart, 1963).
6. For example, Heinz Ladendorf's essay "Kafka und die Kunstgeschichte" (Kafka and Art History), in *Wallraff-Richartz-Jahrbuch,* vol. 25 (1963), pp. 227–62.
7. *Mazes and Labyrinths* was the title of what must be called the classical labyrinth book by William Henry Matthews (London, 1922; reprint New York, 1970).
8. Michael Ayrton, *The Maze Maker* (London: Longmans, 1967). Cf. Nigel Pennick, *Das Geheimnis der Labyrinthe* (The Mystery of the Labyrinths, see note 16), pp. 229f. and the bibliography. Color illustrations in Adrian Fisher's labyrinth book, p. 54 and pp. 146f. (see note 16).
9. Hermann Kern, *Labyrinthe—Erscheinungsformen und Deutungen: 5000 Jahre Gegenwart eines Urbilds* (Labyrinths—Forms and Interpretations: The Five-Thousand-Year Presence of a Primordial Image), 3rd ed. (Munich, 1987).
10. Achille Bonito Oliva, *Im Labyrinth der Vernunft* (In the Labyrinth of

Notes

Reason), p. 54; also here his contribution to the exhibition catalog, "Das Labyrinth als Kunstwerk" (The Labyrinth as Work of Art). See also Achille Bonito Oliva, Paolo Portoghesi, Umberto Eco, and Paolo Sanarcangeli, *Luoghi del silenzio imparziale: Labirinto contemporaneo,* catalog (Milan, 1981).

11. Umberto Eco, *The Name of the Rose* (New York: Harcourt Brace Jovanovich, 1983); first Italian edition, 1980.

12. Friedrich Dürrenmatt, *Labyrinth: Stoffe I–III* (Labyrinth: Matters I–III) (Zurich, 1990), pp. 9–176.

13. Hans Peter Duerr, *Sedna oder Die Liebe zum Leben* (Sedna, or The Love of Life) (Frankfurt, 1990; 1984).

14. Hans Blumenberg, *Höhlenausgänge* (Cave Exits) (Frankfurt, 1989).

15. Manfred Schmeling, *Der labyrinthische Diskurs* (The Labyrinthine Discourse) (Frankfurt, 1987).

16. Two popular introductory works from the English-speaking world, which have appeared in recent years, provide only a limited response to this need. They are: Nigel Pennick, *Mazes and Labyrinths* (London, 1990); and Adrian Fisher and Georg Gerster, *Labyrinth: Solving the Riddle of the Maze* (New York, 1990).

17. According to the *Brockhaus* encyclopedia, the mandala (Skt. "circle," "ring"), in the religions arising out of the Indian culture, is a mystical diagram, which through a concentric arrangement—mostly of a combination of squares and circles—symbolizes the entire cosmos and serves as an image for meditation. Mandalas symbolically represent a religious experience; they are meant to clarify certain spiritual relationships and to lead people who visualize them and meditate upon them to union with the divine. In the depth psychology of C. G. Jung, pictorial representations and dream contents resembling mandalas are interpreted as symbols of self-discovery (individuation).

18. Kern, *Labyrinthe,* p. 13. Here and in subsequent expositions, I follow H. Kern in his elaboration of the concept. See also Kern's concise presentation of his views in *Bild der Wissenschaft,* no. 11 (1982), pp. 148–59.

19. See Kern, *Labyrinthe,* pp. 202f.

20. Ibid. pp. 13–17.

21. In this regard, see also the illustration on p. 15. On the construction of labyrinth figures, see Fisher, *Labyrinth,* pp. 57ff.

22. A critical presentation of this state of affairs is to be found in Geoffrey Stephen Kirk, *The Nature of Greek Myths* (Harmondsworth: Penguin, 1974). On this see also the introduction to Karl Kerényi's narrative work, *Die Mythologie der Griechen* (The Mythology of the Greeks), vol. 1, pp. 7–17. On the problem of reinterpretation, see Fritz Schachermeyr, *Die griechische Rückerinnerung* (The Greek Recollection of the Past), especially on Crete, pp. 281–90.

23. Kern, *Labyrinthe,* figs. 103–104, p. 97.

24. Kern, *Labyrinthe,* pp. 87ff.

25. Ibid., p. 14.

26. Umberto Eco, *Postscript to The Name of the Rose* (New York and San Diego, 1984); more detail can be found in "Kritik des porphyrischen Baumes" (Critique of Porphyry's Tree) in Oliva, *Labyrinth der Vernunft,* pp. 89ff.

27. Ibid., fig. 107, p. 98. A considerably older connection of the classical labyrinth form with figures that could derive from the Theseus saga is documented by the Etruscan wine pitcher from Tragliatella (c. 620 BC). The designation of the Labyrinth as *truia* points to the later labyrinth dance called "Troy Game."

Chapter 1. The Minotaur

Epigraph: Jorge Luis Borges, cited in Bert Nagel, *Kafka und die Weltliteratur* (Kafka and World Literature) (Munich, 1983), p. 363. (As Borges himself explains, it is the Minotaur who fully justifies the existence of the Labyrinth.)

The story is told following Karl Kerényi, *Griechische Mythologie für Erwachsene* (Greek Mythology for Grown-ups), which appeared under the title *Die Mythologie der Griechen* (The Mythology of the Greeks) in two volumes. In the second volume, we encounter our hero again in the stories of heroes. Supplementarily drawn upon were Plutarch's tales of the Cretan journey and the presentation of the same given by Robert Graves.

Chapter 2. The Master Builder

Epigraph: Publius Ovidius Naso, *Metamorphoses* VIII, 157–61.

1. André Gide, "Theseus," in *Two Legends.* Translated by John Russell. (New York: Vintage, 1950).

2. Caption for the labyrinth picture on p. 23 in Kern, *Labyrinthe,* fig. 207, p. 175.

3. Homer, *Ilias* (The Iliad), 18th book, pp. 590ff.

4. Kern, *Labyrinthe,* p. 17.

5. Cf. Hans Peter Duerr, *Sedna oder Die Liebe zum Leben.*

6. See Kern's discussion of Evans's theory, derived from that of the German archaeologist Maximilian Mayer, in Kern, *Labyrinthe,* pp. 46f.

7. See Kern, p. 74.

8. Cited in Kern, p. 72.

9. Vergil, *Aeneis* (Aeneid), V, 588–95 (translation by Eduard Norden).

10. Ibid., VI, 27–30.

11. Ovid, *Metamorphosen* (Metamorphoses), VIII, vv. 161f. (translation by Gerhard Fink), see Chapter 12, note 1.

12. Cf. Wolfgang Haubrich, *Error inextricabilis: Form und Funktion der Labyrinthabbildung in mittelalterlichen Handschriften* (Error Inextrica-

bilis: Form and Function of the Labyrinth Figure in Medieval Manuscripts), in C. Meier and U. Ruberg (eds.), *Text und Bild* (Text and Image) (Wiesbaden, 1980), pp. 63–174, here p. 97: "The single-path construction of the labyrinth so clearly violates the meaning of the figure that the texts repeatedly bring to our attention—the *error* that we must suppose to be a deviation from an intention. The ancient and medieval labyrinth figure represents in diagrammatic form the path, the thread of Ariadne, the conquest the myth celebrates over the *error*—not the construction of the *domus Daedali* with its misleading paths."

Chapter 3. Misunderstandings

Epigraph: Vergil, *Aeneis* (Aeneid), VI, 23–26 (translated by Eduard Norden).

1. The illustration on p. 33 is from the latest version of the *Liber floridus,* which Kern documented in *Labyrinthe,* fig. 189, p. 162; cf. figs. 160 and 161, pp. 160f.

2. The complete Latin text, given in the style usual these days, is as follows: "Pasiphae regina Cretensium concubuit cum tauro induta vaccam ligneam, quam Daedalus ingenio suo composuerat. Concepitque ex eo genuitque minotaurum semivirum et semibovem. Quo nato Daedalus ex praecepto Minois regis fecit foveam, scilicet laberinthum domumque desuper. Positusque est intus minotaurus. Devictis Atheniensibus a Minoe rege Cretensi statuitur illis sibi dari hoc tributum, ut semper post tres annos bis septem corpora iuvenum mitterentur in pastum minotauro. Minos rex iratus adversus Daedalum, tum quia ingenio suo taurum cum Pasiphae regina coire fecerat, tum quia sua indicio Theseus minotaurum occiderat. . . ." (See also in this connection Wolfgang Haubrich, *Error inextricabilis,* pp. 93ff.)

3. *The Iliad* and *The Odyssey* originated in the eighth century B.C. and were written down in the sixth. Their subject matter is Greece's earliest times, the period of migrations and the battles connected with them, which Homer brought to life in poetic form. From about 2000 B.C., Indogermanic tribes migrated into the Mediterranean region. The early Greeks, who were among them and who apparently were known by the name "Achaeans," also invaded Crete and put an end to the Cretan culture around 1450 B.C. (This is questionable according to the most recent research.) The high point of Cretan culture began around 2000 B.C.

4. The following story is based primarily on the account given by Karl Kerényi in *Die Mythologie der Griechen,* vol. 1, chap. 7 (Cretan Stories).

5. Duerr, *Sedna oder Die Liebe zum Leben* (Sedna or The Love of Life), p. 192.

6. See ibid., no. 9, "Der Stier seiner Mutter" (The Bull of His Mother); and no. 10, "Das Zerreissen des Geliebten" (The Dismemberment of the Beloved).

7. Ibid., p. 138. See also on this Mircea Eliade, *Geschichte der religiösen Ideen* (History of Religious Ideas), vol. 1 (Freiburg, 1978), pp. 329f.,

338f.; and Erich Neumann, *Ursprungsgeschichte des Bewussteins* (The Origins and History of Consciousness) (Frankfurt /M., 1984), pp. 71ff.

8. Duerr, p. 191. Duerr compares the two interpretations, the Minoan and the Greek, in a very poignant manner on p. 183.

9. See Eliade, *Geschichte der religiösen Ideen,* vol. 1 (Freiburg, 1978), p. 127.

Chapter 4. Liberation

Epigraph: From Franz Kafka, *Tagebuch* (Diary) for January 24, 1922. Cited from Franz Kafka, *Gesammelte Werke* (Collected Works), Max Brod (ed.), *Tagebücher* (Diaries) 1910–1923, p. 411.

1. Plutarch, *Grosse Griechen und Römer* (Great Greeks and Romans), vol. 1, p. 52.

2. Ibid.

3. See page 46. Caption to figure 620 in Kern, op. cit.

4. For further detail, see Kern, *Labyrinthe,* figs. 644ff, pp. 439ff.

5. Cf. ibid., pp. 430f. That the notion of birth is connected with the windings of the intestines is documented by Kern (ibid., note 8, p. 28) in a reference to Sigmund Freud's *"New Introductory Lectures on Psychoanalysis.* In the twenty-ninth lecture, Freud says: "I cannot fail to mention how often specifically mythological themes are illuminated by dream analysis. For example, the saga of the labyrinth is seen to be a representation of anal birth; the convoluted passages are the intestine, the thread of Ariadne the umbilical cord." (Translated and edited by James Strachey. International Psycho-analytical Library, vol. 24. [London: Hogarth, 1974].)

6. Cf. Stanislav Grof's dramatic account of the recollection of birth, entitled "Urszenen des Austritts" (Primordial Scenes of Exit), in P. Sloterdijk and T. H. Macho (eds.), *Weltrevolution der Seele* (World Revolution of the Soul), vol. 2 (Munich: Artemis & Winkler, 1991), pp. 802ff.

7. Peter Sloterdijk, *Eurotaoismus: Zur Kritik der Politischen Kinetik* (Euro-Taoism: Critique of Political Kinetics), pp. 174f. Under the title of "The Misborn Animal and the Self-Birth of the Subject," Sloterdijk develops a philosophy of birth inspired by Gnosticism. According to his formulation, "Physical birth is the opposite of a coming into the world; it is a falling out of everything familiar, a fall into strangeness, an experience of finding oneself exposed and vulnerable in a bizarre and frightening situation." The "exodus that is birth into the world" means "a voyage of adventure into strange forests." (pp. 174f.)

8. Ibid., p. 176. See also Hans Blumenberg, *Höhlenausgänge,* part 1: "The Caves of Life." Not everyone will be able to put up with E. M. Cioran's book *The Trouble with Being Born,* translated by Richard Howard (New York: Vintage, 1975). In it he speaks of the "catastrophe of birth."

Notes

9. Gernot Böhme has written an excellent book on the phenomenon of Socrates, *Der Typ Socrates* (The Socrates Type) (Frankfurt/M., 1992).

10. Plato's cave simile is worth reading all the way through, and this includes also the interpretation of the simile, which—in contrast to my version— leads right to the center of Plato's philosophy: *The State,* right at the beginning of Book VII. There are many good translations.

   See also, Blumenberg, *Höhlenausgänge,* pp. 83ff. ("Die Höhle in-mitten des Staates") (The Cave in the Middle of the State).

Chapter 5. Rebirth

1. Kern, *Labyrinthe,* picture caption, pp. 320ff.

2. Cf. Karl Kerényi, *Die Mythologie der Griechen* (The Mythology of the Greeks), vol. 2 (The Hero Stories), pp. 183f.

3. René Girard, *Das Heilige und die Gewalt* (The Sacred and Violence) (Zurich, 1987), p. 371.

4. Ibid., p. 370.

5. Michel Leiris, in his chapter "Das Heilige im Alltagsleben" (The Sacred in Everyday Life), in *Die eigene und fremde Kultur* (One's Own and Alien Cultures), vol. 1 (Frankfurt/M., 1985), p. 228. The discussion of the sacred goes back to Rudolf Otto's book *Das Heilige: Über das Irrationale in der Idee des Göttlichen und sein Verhältnis zum Rationalen* (The Sacred: On the Irrational in the Idea of the Divine and its Relationship to the Rational), published in 1917. For a discussion of this concept in the context of the twentieth century, see Adolf Holl, *Im Keller des Heiligtums* (In the Cellar of the Sanctuary) (Stuttgart, 1991), chap. 8, "Gefährliche Heiligkeit" (Dangerous Holiness).

6. A comprehensive presentation with informative graphic material on the theme of Oedipus and the Sphinx is found in Rolf Vogt, *Psychoanalyse zwischen Mythos und Aufklärung oder Das Rätsel der Sphinx* (Psychoanalysis between Myth and Enlightenment or the Riddle of the Sphinx), (Frankfurt/M. and New York, 1986), pp. 49ff.

7. *Lexikon für Theologie und Kirche* (Lexicon for Theology and the Church), vol. 5, 2nd ed. (1965), cols. 674ff.

8. Wolfgang Amadeus Mozart, *The Magic Flute,* Act 2, Scene 28.

9. Mircea Eliade, *Die Sehnsucht nach dem Ursprung* (The Longing for the Origin), p. 155.

10. Cf. Eliade, *Das Mysterium der Wiedergeburt* (The Mystery of Reincarnation) (Zurich and Stuttgart, 1961), p. 16. See also C. G. Jung, *Symbols of Transformation* (*Collected Works,* vol. 5) (Princeton University Press: Princeton, NJ, 1990), pp. 207ff. ("Symbols of the Mother and Rebirth").

11. Kern, *Labyrinthe,* pp. 26ff. On the relationships between ritual, dance, and psychic experience, cf. Neumann, "Zur psychologischen Bedeutung des Ritus, pp. 14ff.

12. See Kern, *Labyrinthe*, fig. 177 (with the representation of the devil in the center).

13. *Lexikon für Theologie und Kirche* (Lexicon for Theology and the Church), vol. 10, cols. 4f. For an amusing yet definitely serious study of the angelic and the demonic, I recommend the richly illustrated work of Malcolm Godwin entitled *Angels: An Endangered Species* (New York, 1990).

14. But the Christian interpretation of the labyrinth is by no means unitary. At least a "double strategy" can be detected. *In bonam partem,* the pattern actualizes the personal union of Christ and Theseus, the process of the Resurrection, the Passion of Christ, the way to Jerusalem, and—according to the interpretation of the Church—the way to the Church and to heaven. *In malam partem,* the labyrinth is the "symbol of sin-ridden entanglement in the world," as, for example, in the representations of the biblical city of Jericho. (Schmeling, *Der Labyrinthische Diskurs*, p. 143, with references to Birkhan and Haubrich.)

15. Alfons Rosenberg, *Die christliche Bildmeditation* (Christian Meditation on Images) (Munich-Planegg, 1955), p. 271.

16. See Chap. 2, n. 12.

17. Romans 6:3,4.

18. On this, see Kern, *Labyrinthe*, pp. 207ff., Hugo Rahner, *Griechische Mythen in christlicher Deutung* (Greek Myths in Christian Interpretation) (Freiburg, 1992), pp. 74ff.

Chapter 6. Concentration

Epigraph: Angelus Silesius, cited following Karl Otto Conrady (ed.), *Das Buch der Gedichte* (The Book of Poems) (Frankfurt/M., 1987), p. 92.

1. Kern, *Labyrinthe*, fig. 274, p. 235.

2. That Christ was a stranger in the world is a basic premise of the New Testament, which derives ultimately from the Jewish idea of the Exodus. The sense of life of the early Christians was formulated in the Epistle to Diognetus (around 200 A.D.): "That strangeness is strange to its fatherland and to any fatherland." This sense of life was lost to a great extent as a result of the turn the Christian Church took under Constantine. Continual reminder of this axiom of Christian life became necessary.

3. As a result of the First Crusade (1096–1099), Jerusalem was conquered in 1099, and the Christian Kingdom of Jerusalem was founded. In 1187, Sultan Saladin reconquered the city, which was also holy to the Muslims. It was not until the Fifth Crusade (1228–1229) that Emperor Frederick II won the holy places of Bethlehem, Nazareth, and Jerusalem back for Christendom through a ten-year peace treaty with Sultan Malek al-Kamil. Jerusalem was already lost again by 1244.

4. Kurt Benesch, *Pilgerwege* (Pilgrim Ways) (Freiburg, 1991), p. 178.

5. Ibid., p. 181.

Notes

6. Ibid., pp. 190f.

7. Cf. Jan van den Meulen and Jürgen Hohmeyer, *Chartres* (Cologne, 1984), pp. 12ff.; Werner Schäfke, *Frankreichs gotische Kathedralen* (France's Gothic Cathedrals), 3rd ed. (Cologne, 1984), pp. 142ff.

8. See illustration on page 74; further details in Kern, *Labyrinthe*, figs. 255–57, pp. 225ff.

9. See illustration on page 72; further details ibid., figs. 278–79, pp. 236ff.

10. Revelations 21:2,3.

11. Revelations 21:5,6. Concerning the interpretation of the center of the labyrinth, the labyrinth of Chartres in all probability did not contain any Minotauromachy, as Hermann Kern made clear in opposition to other views (*Labyrinthe*, picture caption p. 225); it is conceivable that, as in Amiens, the center contained a memorial to the master builder of the cathedral. What seems of greater importance to me is the question of what meaning should be attributed to the six-petaled flower in the center. This is a form that, with the border of the labyrinth in the shape of a toothed wheel, represents a unique feature of Chartres. Kern gives two hints, which might be of further help. The six-petaled flower recalls the tracery of a rose window. This connection is confirmed by Villard de Honnecourt's *Book of Church Masonry*, which has the copies of the labyrinth and the western rose window together on the same page.

12. Cf. Kern, *Labyrinthe*, pp. 214ff.

13. A good overview of this and at the same time a glimpse into the spirit of the new age is given by Ken Wilber in his book *No Boundary: Eastern and Western Approaches to Personal Growth* (Boston: Shambhala, 1980).

    Mircea Eliade sees in the analytic, or therapeutic, process a modern version of what was earlier called initiation. "We could even regard psychoanalysis as a degraded form of initiation, that is, a kind of initiation that is available to a desacralized world. The scenario can still be recognized. The 'descent' into the depths of the psyche, inhabited by 'monsters,' corresponds to the *descensus ad inferos*. The real danger that such a descent holds can be compared to those of typical ordeals of traditional societies, and so on. The result of a successful analysis is the integration of the person, a psychic process, which is not without similarity to the spiritual transformation brought about by genuine initiation." (Mircea Eliade, *Das Mysterium der Wiedergeburt* (The Mystery of Reincarnation), note 57, p. 257.)

14. *Lord of the Underworld* is the title of a work by Colin Wilson on C. G. Jung and the twentieth century.

15. From the "Introduction to the Religious and Psychological Problems of Alchemy," in C. G. Jung, *Psychology and Alchemy, Collected Works* (Princeton, NJ: Princeton University Press, 1980), vol. 12, pp. 6f. Final sentence altered slightly to let the literal meaning, which relates to the present context, come through.

Notes

16. Kern, *Labyrinthe,* note 33, p. 27.

17. Adolf Holl, *Der letzte Christ—Franz von Assisi* (The Last Christian— Francis of Assisi) (Stuttgart, 1979). The historian Georges Duby says about Francis: "This man was, along with Christ, the great hero of Christian history, and one can say without exaggeration that whatever survives of living Christianity today stems from him." (Georges Duby, *Die Zeit der Kathedralen* [The Time of the Cathedrals] [Frankfurt, 1992], p. 245.)

18. Walter Dirks, *Ein zarter, zäher, kleiner Mann* (A Gentle, Tough Little Man), p. 11.

19. Ivan Gobry, *Franz von Assisi* (Hamburg, 1958), p. 35.

20. Johann Baptist Metz, in Kaufmann and Metz, *Zukunftsfähigkeit* (Being Capable of the Future) (Freiburg, 1987), p. 106.

21. Cited following Friedrich Heer, *Europäische Geistesgeschichte* (European Intellectual History), 2nd ed. (Stuttgart, 1965), pp. 204f. The *Fioretti* is found in Francis of Assisi, *Gebete, Ordensregeln, Testament* (Prayers, Rule of the Order, Testament), translated by Wolfram von den Steinen and Max Kirschstein (Zurich, 1979). Cf. also Adolf Holl, *Der letzte Christ,* p. 179.

22. Duby, *Die Zeit der Kathedralen,* p. 230.

23. C. G. Jung, *Psychology and Alchemy, Collected Works,* vol. 12 (Princeton, NJ: Princeton University Press, 1980), p. 7. Jung seems here to continue the critique of Christianity formulated by Søren Kierkegaard almost exactly a hundred years earlier in his "What Is the Difference between an 'Admirer' and a 'Follower' "? (S. Kierkegaard, *Die Leidenschaft des Religiösen* (The Passion of the Religious) (Stuttgart, 1986), pp. 81ff. In contrast to Kierkegaard, the imitation of Christ is obviously understood by Jung as the occurrence of individuation, and Christ has become a symbol of the Self. Cf. C. G. Jung, "Christ, a Symbol of the Self," in *Aion, Collected Works* vol. 9/ii (Princeton, NJ: Princeton University Press, 1978), pp. 36ff.

24. Cf. Hans-Eckehard Bahr, *Mit dem Wolf leben* (Living with the Wolf) (Stuttgart, 1992), p. 74. Bahr treats the new Franciscan culture under the title "Mitfühlen, mitleiden, mitfreuen" (Empathy, Compassion, Shared Joy) and "Freude, schöner Menschen-Funke" (Joy, Beautiful Human Sparks), pp. 28ff.

25. What happened after the death of the revolutionary Francis of Assisi is recounted by Adolf Holl in the last chapter of his book *Der letzte Christ* (Chapter 16, "Nachher" [Afterwards]).

   Umberto Eco gives a gripping fictional account of this aftermath in his novel, *The Name of the Rose,* which is not primarily about the so-called Holy Inquisition but about the poverty movement. Leonardo Boff, who evaded the still-standing regulations of the heritors of the Inquisition in 1992 by leaving the priesthood and the Franciscan order, gave a commentary on the spiritual and also the political content of this novel in his "Die beiden Sackgassen des Bewahrens und des Erschaffens" (The Two

Dead-Ends of Preserving and Creating), in Burkhart Kroeber, *Zeichen in Umberto Ecos Roman "Der Name der Rose"* (Signs in Umberto Eco's Novel "The Name of the Rose") (Munich, 1989), pp. 347ff.

26. For the Reparatus-Basilica in Orléansville, see Kern, *Labyrinthe,* figs. 116–17, p. 119. For San Vitale in Ravenna, see ibid., figs. 276–77, p. 236.

Chapter 7. The World

Epigraph: Kern, *Labyrinthe,* pp. 295f. and fig. 383, p. 303.

1. Friedrich Heer, *Europäische Geistesgeschichte* (European Intellectual History), p. 232.

2. Giovanni Pico della Mirandola, *Über die Würde des Menschen* (On the Dignity of Man), translated by Horst Werner Rüssel (Zurich, 1958), pp. 10f.

3. Kern, *Labyrinthe,* p. 268 (fig. 333 and its caption).

4. Cf. Hugo Rahner, *Griechische Mythen in christlicher Deutung,* reprint (Freiburg, 1992), pp. 77ff.

5. Heer, *Europäische Geistesgeschichte,* p. 241.

6. The first graphic formulation of the maze does not appear until the first half of the fifteenth century (c. 1420) in Italy. The Venetian physician Giovanni Fontana (c. 1395–c. 1455) drew two maze labyrinths in his notebook, one immediately following the other, one round and one rectangular, along with designs for war machines. (Kern, *Labyrinthe,* figs. 235–36; figure in the introduction, p. 14.)

7. Umberto Eco, *Im Labyrinth der Vernunft* (In the Labyrinth of Reason) (Leipzig, 1990), p. 105.

8. Andreas Gryphius, *Es ist alles eitel* (All is Vanity) (1637). See *Das Buch der Gedichte,* edited by K. O. Conrady (Frankfurt/M., 1987), p. 84.

9. Cf. Robert Burton, *The Anatomy of Melancholy.* The first edition of this book, highly successful throughout the seventeenth century, was published in Oxford in 1621.

10. Kern, *Labyrinthe,* p. 234. Cf. Kerényi, *Labyrinthstudien,* p. 246. For the postmodern version, see the epigraph to chapter 10 of the present book from Umberto Eco's *Name of the Rose.*

11. Cited following Veit-Jakobus Dieterich, *Johan Amos Comenius* (Reinbek, 1991), p. 31.

12. Johan Amos Comenius: *Das Labyrinth der Welt und das Paradies des Herzens* (The Labyrinth of the World and the Paradise of the Heart), reprint (Lucerne and Frankfurt/M., 1970), title page. In the Czech title, the German word *Lusthauz* (house of pleasure) is used for "paradise." An interesting insight into the work and influence of this scholar is provided by the catalog of the Bochum Museum for its Comenius Commemorative Exhibit of 1992, *Labyrinth der Welt und Lusthaus des Herzens: J. A. Comenius, 1592–1670.*

13. See illustration on page 92; cf. also Kern, *Labyrinthe*, fig. 374, p. 296.

14. Dmitrij Tschižewskij, *Kleinere Schriften* (Lesser Writings), vol. 2 (Munich, 1972), p. 133.

15. Cf. Kern, *Labyrinthe*, p. 295 and fig. 378, p. 133.

16. Cited following *Kindlers Literatur Lexikon* (Kindler's Lexicon of Literature) (Weinheim, 1981), vol. 6, p. 7506.

17. Tschižewskij, *Kleinere Schriften*, vol. 2, p. 179.

18. Tschižewskij not only presented "Die Thematik und die Quellen des Werks" (The Thematic Background and Sources of the Work [by Comenius]) (*Kleinere Schriften*, vol. 2, pp. 92–139), but also "Die spätere Tradition der Thematik des Labyrinths" (The Later Tradition of the Labyrinth Theme) (ibid., pp. 168–76). In the second essay, he refers, among other works, to Calderon's *Autos sacramentales,* which brought together the traditions of the medieval mystery and morality plays, among them, three in which the themes presented in Comenius's work actually recur in the titles: *El laborinto del mundo, El gran mercado del mundo, El gran teatro del mundo (The Labyrinth of the World, The Great Market of the World, The Great Theater of the World).*

    He missed a work from the Spanish literature of the seventeenth century, which in some parts shows remarkable similarities to Koménski's *Labyrinth of the World,* namely, Baltasar Gracián's *El criticón* (Barcelona: Planeta, 1985). In this work, the big city is not only described as an exemplary labyrinth and true dwelling of the Minotaur, but also specific features of Comenius's presentation crop up in it (upside-down world, catalog of vices, passive observation); German version, pp. 56ff., pp. 74f., pp. 146f.

19. Cf. Tschižewskij, *Kleinere Schriften,* vol. 2, p. 104; and Schmeling, *Der labyrinthische Diskurs,* pp. 145f. While Koménski's *Labyrinth of the World* remained to a great extent unknown, another devotional work of the seventeenth century became one of the most successful books in English literature and one of the most translated works of world literature—John Bunyan's, *Pilgrim's Progress* (Part One, 1678, Part Two, 1684).

20. Cited following Kern, *Labyrinthe,* p. 300.

Chapter 8. The Journey of Life

Epigraph: Daniel Casper von Lohenstein, "Aufschrift eines Labyrinths" (Inscription for a Labyrinth), excerpt; see note 3.

1. See page 97.

2. Baltasar Gracián, *Criticón,* translated by Hanns Studniczka (Hamburg, 1957), p. 74; (the original appeared 1651–57); cf. also Hocke, *Das Labyrinth der Welt,* p. 102; and Bertolt Brecht's poem "Diese babylonische Verwirrung" (This Babylonian Confusion), in *Gesammelte Werke* (Collected Works), vol. 8 (Frankfurt, 1967), pp. 149ff.

3. Daniel Casper von Lohenstein, "Aufschrift eines Labyrinths," in *Frank-*

furter Anthologie, vol. 6, edited by Marcel Reich-Ranicki (Frankfurt, 1982), pp. 27f.

4. Immanuel Kant, "Beantwortung der Frage: Was ist Aufklärung" (Answer to the Question, What is Enlightenment?), in *Werke* (Works), edited by Wilhelm Weischedel (Darmstadt, 1966), vol. 6, pp. 53, 59.

5. Immanuel Kant, *Metaphysik der Sitten: Rechtlehre* (Metaphysics of Morals: Theory of Law), ibid. vol. 4, paras. 28ff., pp. 393ff.

6. Cf. Schmeling, *Der labyrinthische Diskurs,* pp. 140f.

7. Johann Wolfgang Goethe, *Faust I & II,* edited and translated by Stuart Atkins (Cambridge, MA, 1984), p. 1.

8. J. W. Goethe, *Faust,* translated by Philip Wayne (New York, 1959), pp. 133–34.

9. Ibid., pp. 150f.

10. *Wilhelm Meisters Lehrjahre* (The Apprenticeship of Wilhelm Meister), in Goethe, *Werke,* vol. 7. The following quotations are from pp. 86, 494f., 550, 422, 290, 610.

11. Max Kommerell, *Wilhelm Meister;* ibid., p. 364.

12. Novalis, *Werke* (Works), edited by Gerhard Schulz (Munich, 1969), pp. 545f.

13. Ibid., p. 134.

14. Ibid., p. 326.

15. The quotations following this point from the novel *Henry of Ofterdingen* come from chapters 1–4 of part 1; the last comes from part 2.

16. On this point, see Schmeling, *Der labyrinthische Diskurs,* p. 139.

17. Gustav Landauer, cited following Martina Wagner-Egelhaaf, *Mystik der Moderne* (Modern Mysticism) (Stuttgart, 1989), p. 37.

18. Goethe, *Werke,* vol. 7, p. 553.

19. Joseph Freiherr von Eichendorff, *Werke in einem Band* (Works in one volume) (Munich, 1977), pp. 56f.

20. Franz Kafka, *Sämtliche Erzählungen* (Collected Stories), edited by Paul Raabe (Frankfurt/M., 1982), p. 320 ("Kleine Fabel" [Short Fable]).

Chapter 9. The Garden of Love

Epigraph: Johann Wolfgang von Goethe, "Lesebuch" (Reader), a poem in the "Ushk Nameh" (Book of Love), part of *West-östlicher Divan* (West-Eastern Divan; also referred to as *Parliament of West and East),* translation adapted from Johann Wolfgang von Goethe, *West-Eastern Divan,* translated by Edward Dowden (Toronto: J. M. Dent & Sons Ltd., 1914), pp. 35f.

1. 2 Timothy 2:22.

2. Cf. Kern, *Labyrinthe,* chapter 13/4: love labyrinths.

3. 2 Timothy 3:5ff.

4. Cf. Kern, *Labyrinthe* caption for fig. 432.

Notes

5. Michel de Montaigne, *Essais*, I, XXX, cited following Jean-Louis Flandrin, "Das Geschlechtsleben der Eheleute in der alten Gesellschaft: Von der kirchlichen Lehre zum realen Verhalten" (Sex Life of Married People in Earlier Society: From Church Doctrine to Actual Behavior) in *Die Masken des Begehrens und die Metamorphosen der Sinnlichkeit* (Masks of Desire and Metamorphoses of Sensuality), edited by Philippe Ariès and André Béjin (Frankfurt/M., 1992), p. 161.

6. On these, see Kern, *Labyrinthe*, chap. 16, "Trojan Castle and Maidens' Dance"; Nigel Pennick, *Das Geheimnis der Labyrinthe*, pp. 21ff.

7. Cf. Kern, *Labyrinthe*, fig. 596, p. 415. John Kraft, under the title *The Goddess in the Labyrinth* (Åbo, 1995), has presented a wide-ranging interpretation of the "woman in the labyrinth," which agrees in part with our own presentation in chapters 2 and 3 (Åbo, 1985).

8. Pennick, *Das Geheimnis der Labyrinthe*, p. 47 (following Kraft, *Goddess in the Labyrinth*, p. 16).

9. Ibid., p. 48.

10. Joshua 2 and 6.

11. Joshua 2:17ff.

12. One of the stories even has Aphrodite as the companion of Theseus. Cf. Kerényi, *Mythologie der Griechen*, vol. 2, p. 185f.

    The connection of the figure of the labyrinth with the fertility rite of sacred marriage is substantiated by the depictions of the labyrinth in combination with depictions of coitus on the pitcher from Tragliatella (cf. note 27 to the Introduction). The Neolithic cup-and-ring marks are perhaps parallels to this; they show astonishing formal similarities to the megalithic site Stonehenge. Cf. on this Kern *Labyrinthe*, figs. 11–25, pp. 38f.

    On Ariadne Aphrodite, cf. Chapter 2.

13. I would like to recall that the conquest of Crete by the Greeks had as a result an inversion of the hitherto prevailing cultic and mythical situation in the sense of an *interpretatio graeca*. The new hegemony of the phallus led to a reversal of roles in the sacred marriage: Theseus is not the *paredros* of Ariadne, but she is his *paredra*.

14. Walter Burkert, *Griechische Religion der archaischen und klassischen Epoche* (Greek Religion of the Archaic and Classical Periods) (Stuttgart, 1977), pp. 177f.

15. Cf. note 5.

16. Duerr, *Edna*, note 18, pp. 349f.

17. Hocke, *Manierismus, Die Welt als Labyrinth*, p. 180. According to Hocke, the labyrinthine periods belong under the heading of mannerism.

18. Ibid., p. 183.

19. "Die Wollust" (Sensual Pleasure), in *Komm, Zieh dich aus* (Come, Take Off Your Clothes), edited by Heinz-Ludwig Arnold (Zurich, 1991), p. 82.

20. See the epigraph to the previous chapter.

21. Friedrich Schlegel, *Lucinde,* p. 14.

22. Ibid., pp. 20f.

23. Ibid., p. 93.

24. How problematic this model of marriage is can be better judged in retrospect. Cf. on this point Ulrich Beck and Elisabeth Beck-Gernsheim, *Das ganz normale Chaos der Liebe* (The Entirely Normal Chaos of Love), especially chapter 6, "Die irdische Religion der Liebe" (The Earthly Religion of Love) (Frankfurt, 1990).

25. Heinrich Heine, "Lyrical Intermezzo 27," in *Poems of Heinrich Heine,* translated by Louis Untermeyer (New York: Harcourt, Brace, and Company, 1923), p. 58; with slight changes.

26. Johann Wolfgang von Goethe, "Lesebuch" (Reader), a poem in the "Ushk Nameh," a part of *West-östlicher Divan.*

Chapter 10. The Library

Epigraph: Umberto Eco, *The Name of the Rose,* pp. 157f.

1. Kerényi, "Labyrinth-Studien" (Labyrinth Studies), in *Humanistische Seelenforschung* (Munich and Vienna, 1966), p. 243.

2. Cf. Pennick, *Das Geheimnis der Labyrinthe,* p. 224.

3. On the Year of the Labyrinth, see *Caerdroia* (1991), pp. 8ff. The twenty-sixth number of *Caerdroia* (1993) appeared in the summer of 1994. Whoever is interested in this yearly journal should contact the publisher, Jeff Saward, *Caerdroia,* 53 Thundersley Grove, Thundersley, Essex, SS7 3 EB, England, UK. An example of the questionable esoteric direction that the interest in labyrinths seems to be taking in English-speaking countries is the book that appeared in the autumn of 1993 in German translation: Sig Lonegren, *Labyrinthe: Antike Mythen & moderne Nutzungsmöglichkeiten* (Labyrinths: Ancient Myths and Modern Applications) (Glastonbury, 1991; Frankfurt, 1993).

4. Cf. Pennick, *Geheimnis der Labyrinthe,* pp. 235, 237. Color illustrations are to be found in Adrian Fisher's labyrinth book.

   Minotaur Designs had by 1993 constructed more than seventy labyrinths throughout the world. Adrian Fisher is open to newly interested parties. His address is Minotaur Designs, 42 Brompton Road, Saint Alban's, Hertfordshire, AL1 4PT, England, Tel. 44727844800, Fax: . . . 844801.

5. Fisher, *The Riddle of the Maze,* p. 137.

6. Ibid., pp. 148f. (aerial photos with commentary).

7. Cf. Kern, *Labyrinthe,* fig. 4 (Dürer), p. 35.

8. Hocke, *Die Welt als Labyrinth,* pp. 98f.

9. See note to epigraph.

10. Ibid, p. 35.

11. Ibid.

12. Ibid.
13. Ibid., p. 37.
14. Ibid.
15. Ibid., p. 130.
16. Ibid., p. 38.
17. Ibid., p. 215.
18. Ibid., p. 217.
19. Ibid., p. 310.
20. Ibid., p. 320.
21. Ibid. p. 322.
22. Umberto Eco, *Postscript to* The Name of the Rose: "My novel initially bore the working title *The Abbey of Crime*."
23. Eco, *Name of the Rose*, p. 472.
24. Ibid., p. 136.
25. Ibid., p. 112.
26. Ibid., p. 184.
27. Ibid.
28. Ibid., pp. 395f.
29. Ibid.
30. Ibid., p. 399.
31. Ibid.
32. Kant, "Beantwortung der Frage: Was ist Aufklärung?"
33. Eco, *Name of the Rose*, p. 473.
34. Ibid., p. 475.
35. Ibid., p. 477.
36. Horst Fuhrmann, in his introduction to the book of collected essays, "... eine finstere und fast unglaubliche Geschichte?" *Mediävistische Notizen zu Umberto Ecos Mönchsroman "Der Name der Rose"* (A Sinister and Nearly Unbelievable Story?, Medievalist Notes on Umberto Eco's Monastic Novel, *The Name of the Rose*), 3rd ed. (Darmstadt, 1988), p. 5.
37. Jorge Luis Borges, "Die Bibliotek von Babel" (The Library of Babel), in *Gesammelte Werke* (Collected Works), vol. 3/1: Erzählungen (Stories) 1935–1944 (Munich and Vienna, 1981).
38. Ibid.
39. Ibid.
40. Ibid.
41. Ibid.
42. Ibid.
43. Ibid.
44. Ibid.

45. Ibid.

46. Jorge Luis Borges, "Der Garten der Pfade, die sich verweigen" (The Garden of Branching Paths), ibid.

47. Ibid.

48. Ibid.

49. Ibid.

50. On the idea of postmodernism, see Wolfgang Welsch, *Unsere postmoderne Moderne* (Our Postmodern Modernism); 3rd ed. (Weinheim, 1991); particularly with regard to the retrospective view of the Middle Ages, see pp. 57ff.

51. Eco, *Name of the Rose*, p. 14.

52. Ibid., p. 492.

53. Eco, *Nachschrift*, p. 65.

54. Eco, "Die Enzyklopädie als Labyrinth" (The Encyclopedia as Labyrinth), in Eco, *Labyrinth der Vernunft*, p. 106.

55. Gilles Deleuze and Félix Guattari, *Rhizom* (Rhizome) (Berlin, 1977), p. 10.

56. Eco, *Nachschrift*, p. 65.

57. Eco, *Name of the Rose*, p. 491.

58. Cf. Heinz Robert Schlette, "Nur noch nackte Namen . . ." (Just naked names . . .), in *Orientierung*, vol. 12 (1984), pp. 135–38.

59. Eco, *Name of the Rose*, p. 500.

Chapter 11. Prison

Epigraph: "The Labyrinth of Solomon," a poem written in Greek appearing in connection with a drawing of a labyrinth in a composite manuscript of the eleventh century. Cited from Werner Batschelet-Massimi, "Labyrinthzeichnungen in Handschriften" (Labyrinth Drawings in Manuscripts), in *Codices manuscripti*, vol. 4 (1978), part 2, pp. 177–80.

1. Book titles from the 1980s: Wolfgang Welsch, *Unsere postmoderne Moderne* (Our Postmodern Modernism); and Hans-Jürgen Heinrichs, *Die katastrophale Moderne* (Catastrophic Modernism).

2. Ulrich Horstmann, *Das Untier* (The Monster) (Vienna and Berlin, 1983), p. 7.

3. Robert Burton, *Anatomie der Melancholie*, p. 220.

4. B. Gracián, see chapter 8, note 2.

5. Michel Butor, *Der Zeitplan* (The Schedule) (Frankfurt/M., 1989).

6. Friedrich Dürrenmatt, *The Physicists*, translated by James Kirkup (New York: Grove Press, 1964). In his interview with Franz Kreuzer in 1982, Dürrenmatt said, "After all, the play takes place in a madhouse. The madhouse is a further metaphor for the labyrinth." (*Die Welt als Labyrinth:*

Notes

Die Unsicherheit unserer Wirklichkeit [The World as Labyrinth: The Uncertainty of our Reality) (Vienna, 1982), p. 38.

7. Marie Luise Kaschnitz, "Das Labyrinth," in *Engelsbrücke* (Angel's Bridge) (Hamburg: Claasen, 1955).

8. Ibid.

9. Ibid.

10. Ibid.

11. Ibid.

12. Cf. Odo Marquard, "Zeitalter der Weltfremdheit? Beitrag zur Analyse der Gegenwart" (The Age of Alienation from the World? Contribution Toward an Analysis of the Present) in *Philosophie als Zeitdiagnose* (Philosophy as Diagnosis of the Times), edited by Hans-Ludwig Ollig (Darmstadt, 1991), pp. 81–95.

13. Kaufmann and Metz, *Zukunftsfähigkeit* (Being Capable of the Future), pp. 89f.

14. Friedrich Dürrenmatt, *Labyrinth: Stoffe I–III* (Labyrinth: Matters I–III) (Zurich: Diogenes Verlag, 1990), p. 69.

15. Ibid., p. 70.

16. Dürrenmatt, "Der Winterkrieg in Tibet," in *Labyrinth*, pp. 88–176. Cf. on this subject the essay by Gunter E. Grimm, "Dialektik der Ratlosigkeit: Friedrich Dürrenmatt's apokalyptisches Denkspiel *Der Winterkrieg in Tibet*" (The Dialectics of Helplessness: Friedrich Dürrenmatt's Apocalyptic Mental Puzzle *The Winter War in Tibet*, in *Apokalypse*, edited by G. E. Grimm, W. Faul-stich, and P. Kuon (Frankfurt/M., 1986), pp. 313–31.

17. Dürrenmatt, "Der Winterkrieg in Tibet," p. 88.

18. Ibid., p. 89.

19. In his autobiographical "Vorspann" (Leader) to his stories, Dürrenmatt says, "Misled by my *Dramaturgie* (Dramaturgy), I created this about one who I so long believed was the Minotaur, but is Theseus. Only Theseus goes voluntarily, like my mercenary, into the Labyrinth to kill the Minotaur."

20. Dürrenmatt, "Der Winterkrieg in Tibet," p. 98.

21. Ibid., p. 102.

22. Ibid., pp. 103, 118.

23. Ibid., p. 156.

24. Ibid., pp. 160f.

25. Ibid., p. 164.

26. Dürrenmatt, *Bilder und Zeichnungen,* "Persönliche Anmerkung" (Pictures and Drawings, Personal Note) (Zurich-Diogenes, 1978).

27. Friedrich Dürrenmatt, *Minotaurus,* first appeared in 1985.

28. Ibid., pp. 7f.

29. Ibid., p. 13.

30. Ibid., pp. 40f.

31. Ibid., pp. 47f.

32. Ibid., pp. 50f.

33. Friedrich Dürrenmatt, "Das 'Labyrinth' oder Über die Grenzen des Menschseins" ("Labyrinth" or On the Limitations of Being Human) in *Über die Grenzen: Fünf Gespräche* (On Limitations: Five Conversations), edited by Michael Haller (Munich and Zurich, 1983), pp. 99–120.

34. Dürrenmatt, "Der Winterkrieg in Tibet," p. 120.

35. Ulrich Beck, *Risikogesellschaft,* pp. 206f.

36. Ibid., p. 213.

37. Günther Anders, *Die Antiquiertheit des Menschen* (The Antiquatedness of the Human Person), vol. 2 (Munich, 1980), pp. 131–87.

38. Johann Baptist Metz in reference to the book by Robert Bellah et. al., *Habits of the Heart: Individualism and Commitment in American Life* (1985), in Kaufmann and Metz, *Zukunftsfähigkeit,* p. 132.

39. "Ende des Individuums oder Renaissance enormer Subjektivität?" (The End of the Individual or Renaissance of Colossal Subjectivity?), in Beck and Beck-Gernsheim, *Das ganz normale Chaos der Liebe,* p. 61.

40. Ibid., p. 62.

41. Pongs, *Franz Kafka.*

42. Franz Kafka, *The Complete Stories,* edited and translated by Nahum N. Glatzer (New York: Schocken Books, 1971), pp. 325–59.

43. Ibid., pp. 325, 327.

44. Ibid., pp. 331, 333.

45. Ibid., p. 328.

46. Ibid., p. 333.

47. Ibid., p. 327.

48. Ibid., p. 332.

49. Ibid., p. 335.

50. Ibid., p. 340.

51. Ibid., p. 342.

52. Hartmut Binder, *Kafka—Kommentar zu sämtlichen Erzählungen* (Kafka—Commentary to the Collected Stories), 3rd edition (Munich, 1982), p. 322.

53. Kafka, "The Burrow," pp. 348f.

54. Ibid., p. 353.

Chapter 12. Daedalus and Icarus

Epigraph: André Gide, "Theseus," p. 624.

1. Ovid, *Metamorphosen,* p. 189. The account of the Daedalus and Icarus story is based primarily on the version by Robert Graves. Cf. also Hocke, *Manierismus in der Literatur,* pp. 204ff.

Notes

2. Ovid, *Metamorphosen*, Book VIII, lines 225–33, p. 190.
3. Gide, "Theseus," p. 624. In Gide's story Daedalus gives Theseus the information about the Labyrinth and tells him the story of Icarus before (!) Theseus goes into the Labyrinth.
4. Virgil, *The Aeneid*, translated by Robert Fitzgerald (New York: Vintage Books, 1990), Book VI, lines 47–50, p. 160.
5. Hocke, *Manierismus in der Literatur*, p. 285.
6. On the following, cf. Joseph Leo Koerner, *Die Suche nach dem Labyrinth* (The Quest for the Labyrinth) (Frankfurt/M., 1983), especially pp. 117ff.
7. Sebastian Brant, "Das Narrenschiff" (The Ship of Fools) (Stuttgart, 1992), p. 145f.
8. John Milton, *Paradise Lost*, first appeared 1667.
9. Cf. Beat Wyss, *Pieter Bruegel, Landschaft mit Ikarussturz: Ein Vexierbild des humanistischen Pessimissmus* (Pieter Brueghel's "Landscape with Fall of Icarus," a Picture Puzzle of Humanistic Pessimism) (Frankfurt/M., 1993). The date given for the painting varies between 1555 and 1569.
10. Marie Luise Kaschnitz, *Wohin denn ich? Aufzeichnungen* (So Where Do I Go? Notes) (Hamburg, 1963), p. 69.
11. W. H. Auden, "Musée des Beaux Arts," in *Collected Poems*, edited by Edward Mendelson (London: Faber & Faber, 1976), pp. 146f.

Bibliography

Anders, Günther. *Die Antiquiertheit des Menschen.* Vol. 2: *Über die Zerstörung des Lebens im Zeitalter der dritten industriellen Revolution.* Munich, 1980.

Arnold, Heinz-Ludwig (ed.). *Komm. Zieh dich aus: Handbuch der lyrischen Hocherotik deutscher Zunge.* Zurich, 1991.

Auden, W. H. *Collected Poems.* Edited by Edward Mendelson. London: Faber & Faber, 1976.

Ayrton, Michael. *The Maze Maker.* London: Longmans, 1967.

Bahr, Hans-Eckehard. *Mit dem Wolf leben.* Stuttgart, 1992.

Batschelet-Massimi, Werner. "Labyrinthzeichnungen in Handschriften." In *Codices manuscripti,* vol. 4/2 (1978), pp. 33–65.

Beck, Ulrich, and Elisabeth Beck-Gernsheim. *Das ganz normale Chaos der Liebe.* Frankfurt/M.: Suhrkamp, 1990.

Benesch, Kurt. *Pilgerwege: Santiago de Compostela.* With color illustrations by Rudolf Tiessler. Freiburg, 1991.

Binder, Hartmut. *Kafka—Kommentar zu sämtlichen Erzählungen.* 3rd ed. Munich, 1982.

Blumenberg, Hans. *Höhlenausgänge.* Frankfurt/M.: Suhrkamp, 1989.

Böhme, Gernot. *Der Typ Sokrates.* Frankfurt/M.: Suhrkamp, 1992.

Borges, Jorge Luis. "Die Bibliothek von Babel," in *Gesammelte Werke.* Vol. 3/1: *Erzählungen 1935–1944.* Translated by Karl A. Horst and Curt Meyer-Clason. Munich and Vienna: Hanser, 1981.

———. *Labyrinths.* Modern Library, 1964.

———. *Obras completas.* 2 vols. Buenos Aires: Emece, 1989.

Brant, Sebastian. *Das Narrenschiff.* Stuttgart: Reclam, 1992.

Brecht, Bertolt. *Gesammelte Werke.* Vol. 8. Frankfurt/M.: Suhrkamp, 1967.

Das Buch der Gedichte: Deutsche Lyrik von den Anfängen bis zur Gegenwart. Edited by Karl Otto Conrady. Frankfurt/M., 1987.

Bunyan, John. *The Pilgrim's Progress.* New York: Charles Scribner's Sons, 1895.

Burkert, Walter. *Griechische Religion der archaischen und klassischen Epoche.* Stuttgart, 1977.

Burton, Robert. *The Anatomy of Melancholy.* Edited by Thomas C. Faulkner, Nicolas K. Kiessling, and Rhonda L. Blair. 2 vols. New York: Oxford University Press, 1989.

Butor, Michel. *Der Zeitplan.* Frankfurt/M.: Suhrkamp, 1989.

Caerdroia: The Journal of Mazes & Labyrinths. 1991ff.

Bibliography

Cioran, E. M. *The Trouble with Being Born: A Short History of Decay*. Translated by Richard Howard. New York: Viking, 1975.

———. *La tentation d'exister*. Paris: Gallimard, 1995.

Comenius, Johann Amos. *Das Labyrinth der Welt und das Paradies des Herzens*. Lucerne and Frankfurt/M., 1971.

———. *The Labyrinth of the World and the Paradise of the Heart*. Translated by Matthew Spink. Ann Arbor: University of Michigan Press, 1972.

Deleuze, Gilles, and Félix Guattari. *Rhizom*. Berlin, 1977.

———. *Rhizome*. Paris: Editions de Minuit, 1976.

Dieterich, Veit-Jacobus. *Johann Amos Comenius*. Reinbek: Rowohlt, 1991.

Dirks, Walter. *Ein zarter, zäher, kleiner Mann*.

Duby, Georges. *Die Zeit der Kathedralen: Kunst und Gesellschaft 980–1420*. Frankfurt/M.: Suhrkamp, 1992.

Duerr, Hans Peter. *Sedna oder Die Liebe zum Leben*. Frankfurt/M.: Suhrkamp, 1990.

Dürrenmatt, Friedrich. *Bilder und Zeichnungen*. Edited by Christian Strich. With an Introduction by Manuel Gasser and a Commentary by Friedrich Dürrenmatt. Zurich: Diogenes, 1978.

———. *Labyrinth: Stoffe I–III*. Zurich: Diogenes, 1990.

———. *Minotaurus: Eine Ballade*. With illustrations by the author. Zurich: Diogenes, 1985.

———. *The Physicists*. Translated by James Kirkup. New York: Grove, 1964.

———. *Über die Grenzen: Fünf Gespräche*. Edited by Michael Haller. Munich and Zurich, 1993.

Eco, Umberto. *Im Labyrinth der Vernunft: Texte über Kunst und Zeichen*. Leipzig, 1990.

———. *The Name of the Rose*. New York and San Diego: Harcourt Brace Jovanovich, 1983.

———. *Postscript to* The Name of the Rose. New York and San Diego: Harcourt Brace Jovanovich, 1984.

Eichendorff, Joseph Freiherr von. *Werke in einem Band*. Bibliothek deutscher Klassiker, vol. 32. Munich, 1977.

Eliade, Mircea. *Geschichte der religiösen Ideen*. Vol. 1: *Von der Steinzeit bis zu den Mysterien von Eleusis*. Freiburg, 1978.

———. *History of Religious Beliefs and Ideas*. Translated by Willard R. Trask. Chicago: University of Chicago Press, 1978.

———. *Das Mysterium der Wiedergeburt: Initiationsriten, ihre kulturelle und religiöse Bedeutung*. Zurich and Stuttgart, 1961.

———. *Die Sehnsucht nach dem Ursprung: Von den Quellen der Humanität*. Frankfurt/M.: Suhrkamp, 1989.

Fisher, Adrian, and Georg Gerster. *Labyrinth: Solving the Riddle of the Maze*. New York, 1990.

Flandrin, Jean-Louis. "Das Geschlechtsleben der Eheleute in der alten Gesellschaft: Von der kirchlichen zum realen Verhalten." In Philippe Ariès and André Béjin (eds.), *Die Masken des Begehrens und die Metamorphosen der Sinnlichkeit: Zur Geschichte der Sexualität im Abendland*. Frankfurt/M.: Fischer, 1992.

Bibliography

Francis of Assisi. *Gebete, Ordensregelen, Testament.* Translated by Wolfram von den Steinen and Max Kirschstein. Zurich, 1979.

Frankfurter Anthologie. Vol. 6. Edited by Marcel Reich-Ranicki. Frankfurt/M.: Insel, 1982.

Freud, Sigmund. *New Introductory Lectures on Psycho-analysis.* Translated and edited by James Strachey. International Psycho-analytical Library, vol. 24. London: Hogarth Press, 1974.

Fuhrmann, Horst (ed.). *".* . . *eine finstere und fast unglaubliche Geschichte"? Mediävistische Notizen zu Umberto Ecos Mönchsroman "Der Name der Rose."* 3rd ed. Darmstadt, 1988.

Gide, André. *Two Legends: Oedipus and Theseus.* Translated by John Russell. New York: Vintage, 1950.

Girard, René. *Das Heilige und die Gewalt.* Zurich, 1987.

Gobry, Ivan. *Franz von Assisi—mit Selbstzeugnissen und Bilddokumenten.* Hamburg, 1958.

Godwin, Michael. *Angels: An Endangered Species.* New York: Simon & Schuster, 1990.

Goethe, Johann Wolfgang von. *Faust.* Translated by Philip Wayne. New York: Penguin, 1959.

———. *Faust I & II.* Translated by Stuart Atkins. Cambridge, Mass.: Suhrkamp, 1984.

———. *West-Eastern Divan.* Translated by Edward Dowden. Toronto: J. M. Dent & Sons, 1914.

———. *Wilhelm Meisters Lehriahre.* In *Werke.* Vol. 7. Hamburger Ausgabe, 1949ff.

Gracián, Baltasar. *El criticón.* Barcelona: Planeta, 1985.

———. *Criticón oder Über die allgemeinen Laster der Menschen.* Translated by Hanns Studniczka. Hamburg, 1957.

Graves, Robert. *The Greek Myths.* Mt. Kisco, N.Y.: Moyer Bell, 1988.

Grimm, Gunter E. "Dialektik der Ratlosigkeit: Friedrich Dürrenmatts apokalyptisches Denkspiel *Der Winterkrieg in Tibet.*" In Grimm, W. Faulstich, and P. Kuon (eds.), *Apokalypse.* Frankfurt/M.: Suhrkamp, 1986, pp. 313–31.

Haubrich, Wolfgang. *Error inextrabilis: Form und Funktion der Labyrinthabbildung in mittelalterlichen Handschriften.* In Christel Meier and Uwe Ruberg (eds.), *Text und Bild: Aspekte des Zusammenwirkens zweier Künste in Mittelalter und früher Neuzeit.* Wiesbaden, 1980.

Heer, Friedrich. *Europäische Geistesgeschichte.* 2nd ed. Stuttgart, 1965.

Heine, Heinrich. *Poems of Heinrich Heine.* Translated by Louis Untermeyer. New York: Harcourt, Brace, 1923.

Heinrichs, Hans-Jürgen. *Die katastrophale Moderne.* Frankfurt/M. and Paris, 1984.

Hocke, Gustav René. *Die Welt als Labyrinth: Manier und Manie in der europäischen Kunst.* Hamburg: Rowohlt, 1957.

———. *Manierismus in der Literatur: Sprach-Alchimie und esoterische Kombinationskunst.* Hamburg: Rowohlt, 1959.

Bibliography

Holl, Adolf. *Im Keller des Heiligtums:* Geschlecht und Gewalt in der Religion. Stuttgart, 1991.

———. *Der letzte Christ—Franz von Assisi.* Stuttgart, 1979.

Horstmann, Ulrich. *Das Untier.* Vienna and Berlin, 1983.

Jung, Carl Gustav. *Aion. Collected Works.* Vol. 9/ii. Princeton, N.J.: Princeton University Press, 1978.

———. *Psychology and Alchemy. Collected Works.* Vol. 12. Princeton, N.J.: Princeton University Press, 1980.

———. *Symbols of Transformation. Collected Works.* Vol. 5. Princeton, N.J.: Princeton University Press, 1967.

Kafka, Franz. *The Complete Stories.* Edited and translated by Nahum N. Glatzer. New York: Schocken, 1971.

———. *Sämtliche Erzählungen.* Edited by Paul Raabe. Frankfurt/M.: Fischer, 1982.

———. *Tagebücher 1910–1923.* In *Gesammelte Werke.* Edited by Max Brod. Frankfurt/M.: Fischer, 1983.

Kant, Immanuel. *Metaphysik der Sitten: Rechtslehre.* In *Werke.* Edited by Wilhelm Weischedel. Vol. 4. Darmstadt, 1966.

———. "Beantwortung der Frage: 'Was ist Aufklärung?'" In *Werke.* Edited by Wilhelm Weischedel. Vol. 6. Darmstadt, 1966.

Kaschnitz, Marie Luise. *Griechische Mythen.* Munich: Deutscher Taschenbuch Verlag, 1975.

———. "Das Labyrinth." In *Engelsbrücke.* Hamburg: Claassen, 1955.

———. *Wohin denn ich? Aufzeichnungen.* Hamburg: Claassen, 1963.

Kaufmann, Franz-Xaver and Johann Baptist Metz. *Zukunftsfähigkeit: Suchbewegungen im Christentum.* Freiburg, 1987.

Kerényi, Karl. "Labyrinth-Studien." In *Humanistische Seelenforschung.* Munich and Vienna, 1966, pp. 226–73.

———. *Die Mythologie der Griechen.* Vol. 1: *Die Gütter- und Menschheitsgeschichten.* Vol. 2: *Die Heroen-Geschichten.* Munich, 1966.

Kern, Hermann. *Labyrinthe—Erscheinungsformen und Deutungen: 5000 Jahre Gegenwart eines Urbilds.* 3rd ed. Munich: Prestel, 1987.

———. "Das Labyrinth: Geheimnis zwischen Tod und Wiedergeburt." In *Bild der Wissenschaft,* vol. 11 (1982), pp. 148–59.

Kierkegaard, Søren. *Die Leidenschaft des Religiösen: Eine Auswahl aus Schriften und Tagebüchern.* Stuttgart: Reclam, 1986.

Kirk, Geoffrey Stephen. *Griechische Mythen: Ihre Bedeutung und Funktion.* Reinbek: Rowohlt, 1987.

Koerner, Leo. *Die Suche nach dem Labyrinth: Daedalus, Ikarus und das Labyrinth.* Frankfurt/M., 1983.

Kraft, John. *The Goddess in the Labyrinth.* Åbo, 1985.

Kreuzer, Franz. *Die Welt als Labyrinth: Die Unsicherheit unserer Wirklichkeit—Franz Kreuzer im Gespräch mit Friedrich Dürrenmatt und Paul Watzlawick.* Vienna, 1982.

Kroeber, Burkhart (ed.). *Zeichen in Umberto Ecos Roman 'Der Name der Rose.'* Munich: Deutscher Taschenbuch Verlag, 1989.

Bibliography

Ladendorf, Heinz. "Kafka und die Kunstgeschichte II." In *Wallraff-Richartz-Jahrbuch,* vol. 25 (1963), pp. 227–62.

Leiris, Michel. *Die eigene und die fremde Kultur: Ethnologische Schriften.* Vol. 1. Frankfurt/M.: Suhrkamp, 1985.

Lexikon für Theologie und Kirche. 2nd ed. 1957ff.

Lonegren, Sig. *Labyrinthe: Antike Mythen und moderne Nutzungsmöglichkeiten.* Frankfurt, 1993.

Odo Marquard. "Zeitalter der Weltfremdheit? Beitrag zur Analyse der Gegenwart." In Hans-Ludwig Ollig (ed.), *Philosophie als Zeitdiagnose.* Darmstadt, 1991.

Matthews, William Henry. *Mazes and Labyrinths: Their History and Development.* 1922. Reprint. New York, 1970.

Nagel, Bert. *Kafka und die Weltliteratur: Zusammenhänge und Wechselwirkungen.* Munich, 1983.

Novalis. *Werke.* Edited by Gerhard Schulz. Munich, 1969.

Oliva, Achille Bonito, Paolo Portoghesi; Umberto Eco; and Paolo Sanarcangeli. *Luoghi des silenzio imparziale: Labirinto contemporaneo.* Milan, 1981.

Ovid. *Metamorphosen: Das Buch der Mythen und Verwandlungen.* Translated by Gerhard Fink. Frankfurt/M.: Fischer, 1992.

Pennick, Nigel. *Das Geheimnis der Labyrinthe: Eine Reise in die Welt der Irrgärten.* Munich: Goldmann, 1992.

———. *Mazes and Labyrinths.* London, 1990.

Pico della Mirandola, Giovanni. *Über die Würde des Menschen.* Translated by Horst Werner Rüssel. Zurich, 1958.

Plutarch. *Vitae parallelae/Parallel Lives.* With an English translation by Bernadotte Perin. Cambridge: Harvard University Press, 1982.

Pongs, Hermann. *Franz Kafka: Dichter des Labyrinths.* Heidelberg, 1960.

Rahner, Hugo. *Griechische Mythen in christlicher Deutung.* Reprint. Freiburg: Herder, 1992.

Rosenberg, Alfons. *Die christliche Bildmeditation.* Munich-Planegg, 1955.

Schachermeyer, Fritz. *Die griechische Rückerinnerung im Lichte neuer Forschungen.* Vienna, 1983.

Schäfke, Werner. *Frankreichs gotische Kathedralen: Eine Reise zu den Höhepunkten mittelalterlicher Architektur in Frankreich.* 3rd ed. Cologne, 1984.

Schlette, Heinz Robert. " 'Nur noch nackte Namen . . .': überlegungen zu Umberto Eco: *Der Name der Rose.* In *Orientierung,* vol. 12 (1984), pp. 135–38.

Schmeling, Manfred. *Der labyrinthische Diskurs: Vom Mythos zum Erzählmodell.* Frankfurt/M., 1987.

Sloterdijk, Peter, and Thomas H. Macho (eds.). *Weltrevolution der Seele: Ein Lese- und Arbeitsbuch der Gnosis von der Spätantike bis zun Gegenwart.* 2 vols. Munich: Artemis & Winkler, 1991.

Thalmann, Marianne. *Romantik und Manierismus.* Stuttgart, 1963.

Tschizewskij, Dmitrij. *Kleinere Schriften.* Vol. 2. Munich: Bohemica, 1972.

Bibliography

Van den Meulen, Jan, and Jürgen Hohmeyer. *Chartres: Biographie einer Kathedrale.* Cologne, 1984.

Virgil. *The Aeneid.* Translated by Robert Fitzgerald. New York: Vintage, 1990.

Vogt, Rolf. *Psychoanalyse zwischen Mythos und Aufklärung oder Das Rätsel der Sphinx.* Frankfurt/M. and New York, 1986.

Wagner-Engelhaaf, Martina. *Mystik der Moderne.* Stuttgart, 1989.

Welsch, Wolfgang. *Unsere postmoderne Moderne.* 3rd ed. Weinheim, 1991.

Wilber, Ken. *No Boundary: Eastern and Western Approaches to Personal Growth.* Boston: Shambhala Publications, 1980.

Wilson, Colin. *The Lord of the Underworld: Jung and the Twentieth Century.* Wellingborough, N.H.: Aquarius, 1984.

Wyss, Beat. *Pieter Bruegel, Landschaft mit Ikarussturz: Ein Vexierbild des humanistischen Pessimismus.* Frankfurt/M.: Fischer, 1993.

Index

Index

Brant, Sebastian, 152
Bronze Age, 10
Brueghel, Pieter, 154
bull. *See also* Minotaur; bull games
in León, 115; Bull of Marathon,
18; Bull of Minos, 26, 113, 115;
Minos as, 38, 40; in mythology,
26, 39, 40; Pasiphae's liaison with,
35, 36; sent by Poseidon, 36, 40
Burton, Robert, 135
"bush time," 58
Butor, Michel, 135

*Caerdroia: The Journal of Mazes and
Labyrinths,* 120
cathedrals, significance of, 30, 73–
74. *See also* church labyrinths
cave; cavewomb of Great Goddess,
39; of Cretan Zeus, 40; in Dürrenmatt's *The Winter War in Tibet,*
139–140; as existential symbol, 4;
labyrinth as, 35, 45; on Mount
Dicte, 38, 41; in Novalis's *Henry
of Ofterdingen,* 102, 103, 104;
Plato's simile of, 49–50
centaur, Minotaur depicted as, 25
center of labyrinth. *See also* middle;
in Chartres, 73, 74; Christ in, 68,
69, 78; Cretan, 7, 17; devil in, 61;
"holy church" as, 82; as interior
(Jung), 77; modern labyrinths and,
89; as path into the depths, 105; as
self-reflection, 87; Theseus's encounter in, 56–58, 59
chaos, initiatory death and, 59
Chartres, cathedral of, 72–73, 77
childhood, 48
Christ; celebration of resurrection,
77; Francis of Assisi and, 80; in
rose window in Chartres, 75; in
The Labyrinth of the World, 94,
95; as the new Theseus, 61, 64, 68
Christianity; labyrinth symbolism
and, 61, 63–65; medieval, 78, 79,
81; Reformation, 89–90, 95
church labyrinths; in Cathedral of
Amiens, 65; in Cathedral of San

Martino (Lucca), 54; in church of
San Pietro de Conflentu (Pontrem-
oli), 68; in church of San Savino in
Piacenza, 90; in church of Sibbo
(Finland), 110; in Notre Dame de
Chartres, 72–73; in Notre Dame
de Reims, 73; in Reparatus Basilica
of Orléansville, 82; in San Vitale in
Ravenna, 82; symbolism of, 76,
81–82
city; "City of Troy," 120–121; Holy
City (Rome), 70; as labyrinth, 30–
31, 91, 135; metaphor for the
world, 95
closet of mirrors, 87–88, 141, 143
Coate, Randoll (maze designer), 121,
122
Cocalus, King of Sicily, 151, 152
Comenius, 91, 95, 135
Compostela, 70, 71–72, 79
concentration; church labyrinths
and, 76; medieval pilgrimage sites
and, 70, 71
confusion, 89
convolutions; crane dance patterns,
59; as hurdles in Christian life, 69;
number of, 7, 34, 45, 63
cosmic knot, 123
"cosmic labyrinth," 137
cow; Daedalus's creation, 42, 148; in
early Mediterranean mythology,
26; Pasiphae as, 36, 38
Cretan Labyrinth. *see also* Ariadne;
Daedalus; Minotaur; Theseus; archaeological finds and, 10, 12; and
church labyrinths compared, 63;
Daedalus's depiction of, 151; as
Daedalus's prison, 148–149; in
medieval manuscripts, 34; mythology surrounding, 5, 8, 16–22, 26;
Pliny's model for, 28; as sacred
dance site, 25–26
Crete; absence of labyrinth building
on, 26–27; ancient mythology of,
38, 40; Daedalus and, 17, 150;
Theseus's voyage to, 54–55
crisis, postmodern, 134

Index

Index

Knossos; palace of, 27; in Labyrinth
story, 16, 18, 55
knots, 123, 131
knowledge; at center of labyrinth, 78;
in *The Name of the Rose*, 126–127
Koménsky, Jan Amos (Comenius),
91, 95, 135

Labyrinth of Flirtation, 108, 109
Labyrinth of the World, The (Comenius) 91–95
Lady of the Labyrinth, 25, 26
Lambert, of Saint-Omer, 34, 35
Lappa Maze, 121
lawn mazes, English, 31
liberation; of Athenian youths, 21,
56; from childhood, 48–49; from
Hell, 61; into open space, 47; in
Plato's cave simile, 50; of world,
61; of young woman, 111
Liber floridus (Lambert); Cretan
Labyrinth in, 34, 35; Labyrinth
mythology in, 41, 42
library; and insane asylum compared,
136; in *The Name of the Rose*,
124–126, 128–130
literature, labyrinth in, 4–6, 91, 99,
116, 123. *See also individual authors*
love labyrinths, 108, 116; in Europe,
109–110; Goethe's and, 117
Lucca, Italy, 54
Lucinde (in Schlegel's *Lucinde*) 116
Luther, Martin, 89
Luzzanas (Sardinia), 8, 10

Magna Mater, 39
males, Labyrinth stories and, 13, 155
mandala, labyrinth as, 5, 13–14
"maps of mystery," 123
Marino, Gianbattista, 115, 117
marriage; de Montaigne's view of,
113–114; *hierosgamos*, 39, 40,
113; and love labyrinths, 108, 109;
Romantics' understanding of, 116,
117
Matthews, William Henry, 120

maturity; of Henry (in *Henry of Ofterdingen*), 104; of young adult, 49
maze; Daedalus's Labyrinth as, 29; of
defense, 128; designers, 121–123;
Egyptian labyrinth as, 28; English
lawn mazes, 31; in *Henry of Ofterdingen*, 102; labyrinth as, 5–6,
88–89; modern labyrinthine state
of affairs, 116; spiritual, 96; symbolic of melancholy, 90
Metamorphoses (Ovid), 28–29, 149–
150
middle. *See also* center; Castle Keep
(in Kafka's "The Burrow"), 144;
of labyrinth dance, 26, 60; of library labyrinth, 125–126, 128; of
"Trojan Castles," 110–111
Middle Ages; in Eco's *The Name of
the Rose*, 129; manuscripts from,
34–35; pilgrimage sites in, 68–73;
Theseus as hero in, 54
Miller, Henry, 115
Milton, John, 153
Minoan Labyrinth. *See* Cretan Labyrinth
Minos, King of Crete, 16; Athens
subjugated by, 18; as a bull, 38,
40; in Cretan mythology, 26; and
Daedalus, 17, 148, 151–152; death
of, 152; deceived by Ariadne, 21;
divine origins of, 38; Greek accounts of, 40, 55; and Poseidon,
36; Theseus representing, 113
Minotaur; Athenians and, 18, 44;
Christianization of, 68; classical
name of, 40; in Cretan accounts,
26, 44, 45; depicted in *Liber floridus*, 34; as discord and concord,
116; Daedalus and, 42; driven out
of womb, 47; Dürrenmatt's, 139,
140–142; in Gide's story, 24; Kafka's, 144–146; killed by Theseus,
18–20, 54, 142; labyrinth symbolism and, 12–13, 17, 89; medieval
interpretation of, 61; as *monstrum
sacrum*, 56–58; Pasiphae's son, 16,
38; Plato's cave simile and, 50–51;

189

Index

Minotaur (*continued*)
  in Pliny's work, 27; and Theseus as
  one, 140–142; today's "single" as,
  143–144
Minotaur Designs, 121
mirror closet, 87–88, 141, 143
modernism, "catastrophic," 134
monasticism; medieval Christian, 69,
  79, 81; in *The Name of the Rose*,
  123–124
monster; love as "modern monster,"
  115; Minotaur as *monstrum sacrum*, 56– 58; Ulrich's, 135
Monteverdi, Claudio, opera of, 13
mosaics, labyrinth depictions, 82, 90
Mother Earth, 39; cult of dead and,
  10; labyrinth as symbol, 45; and
  Virgin Mary compared, 68
Mount Dicte, cave on, 38, 41
movement, labyrinth and, 77
Müntzer, Thomas, 89
music, operas inspired by Ariadne,
  13
mythology; of ancient Crete, 38, 40;
  of Asia, 38; of Cretan Labyrinth,
  8, 16–22, 26; Greeks' interpretation of, 26, 35–36, 40–41, 42

Name of the Rose, The (Eco), 4, 123–
  129, 131–132
Native Americans, Hopi, 45
Naxos (Dia), isle of, 20–21, 149
new age, Renaissance as, 87
Newquay Zoo, "Dragon Labyrinth"
  in, 121
Novalis, 101–104

octagon, 65, 83, 87
Oedipus, 56, 57, 58
operas, inspired by Ariadne, 13
Orwellian year (1984), 134, 135
Ovid, 28, 149

Paradise, 61, 109
paredros (companion), 39, 40, 113
Pasiphae; absent in post-Labyrinthine tales, 155; in Cretan mythol-

ogy, 26, 40; Daedalus and, 42,
  148; divine origins of, 35–36, 38;
  as goddess, 113; in Lambert's account, 35–36; as Minotaur's
  mother, 16, 38
paths; dance movement and, 120;
  into daylight, 51; false, 5, 89; into
  interior, 105; in psychology,
  77–79; single path, 7, 29; straying,
  116; in *The Labyrinth of the
  World*, 95; into world, 47, 58
patterns; convolutions, 7, 34, 45, 63;
  of crane dance, 59
Perseis, Pasiphae as daughter of, 36
petroglyphs, 8, 10
Philochoros, 44
Pia desideria (Hugo), 95, 96
Pico della Mirandola, Giovanni, 87
pilgrimage; of Francis of Assisi, 79;
  in Koménsky's works, 93, 94;
  meaning of, 76, 83; in medieval
  Christian life, 69, 71; in Novalis's
  works, 101–102; pilgrimage sites,
  68–73
Plato, 49
Pliny, 27, 28, 29
"poet of the labyrinth," 2, 144
Polycaste (Daedalus's sister), 150
Pompeii, archaeological find in, 10,
  12
Pontremoli, archaeological find in,
  68, 79
Poseidon; revenge against King
  Minos, 36; sacrificial bull of, 40;
  Theseus and, 55
postmodernism, 131
prison; Daedalus's, 148, 152; Kafkan
  Minotaur's fear as, 146; for Minotaur, 17, 44, 45; postmodern labyrinth as, 136, 137; society as,
  143–144; for young woman, 111
Proteus (in *Faust*), 100
psychology, 47–49, 77–79
puberty, 49
Pylos, archaeological find in, 8

Rahab, thread of, 111
rebirth; Christian baptism as, 88;

Credits

Text

Excerpts from "The Labyrinth" from *Wohin denn ich: Aufzeichnungen* by Marie-Luise Kaschnitz, ©1983 by Claassen Verlag, Hildesheim, Germany, Reprinted by permission.

Excerpts from "The Winter War in Tibet" from *Stoffe I–III* by Friedrich Dürrenmatt, © 1990 by Diogenes Verlag AG, Zurich, Switzerland. Reprinted by permission.

Excerpts from "The Burrow" from *Franz Kafka: The Complete Stories* by Franz Kafka, edited by Nahum Glatzer, © 1946, 1947, 1948, 1949, 1954, 1958, 1971 by Schocken Books, Inc. Reprinted by permission of Schocken Books, published by Pantheon Books, a division of Random House, Inc.

Excerpts from *The Name of the Rose* by Umberto Eco, © 1980 by Gruppo Editoriale Fabbri-Bompioni, Sonzogno, Etas S.p.A., English translation © 1983 by Harcourt Brace & Company and Martin Secker & Warburg Limited. Reprinted by permission of Harcourt Brace & Company and of Reed Consumer Books Ltd.

Excerpt from "Musée des Beaux Arts" from *Collected Poems* by W. H. Auden, edited by Edward Mendelson. © 1940 and renewed 1968 by W. H. Auden. Reprinted by permission of Random House, Inc., and Faber and Faber Ltd.

Illustrations

Bull labyrinth from *Die Zeit,* no. 8 (February 19, 1993).

Arkville Maze and *Lappa Maze, Cornwall:* Courtesy of the Armand G. Erpf Fund, New York City. Used by permission of Georg Gerster, Zumikon-Zürich, Switzerland.

Lucca: courtesy of Dr. Wilfried Kerndtke, Offenbach, Germany.

Theseus and Ariadne, Theseus Fights against Minotaurus, and *Attended by Ariadne, Theseus Fights against Minotaurus:* Courtesy of Hirmer Verlag GmbH, Munich, Germany.

Labyrinth III: from *Bilder und Zeichnungen* by Friedrich Dürrenmatt, © 1978 by Diogenes Verlag AG, Zurich, Switzerland.

Minotaur: from *Mintoraurus* by Friedrich Dürrenmatt, © 1985 by Diogenes Verlag AG, Zurich, Switzerland.